AT HOME WITH TOWN & COUNTRY

AT HOME WITH TOWN & COUNTRY

SARAH MEDFORD

HEARST BOOKS

New York

CONTENTS

The Benetton family
in Italy.

OVERLEAF: The Los
Angeles courtyard of
Frances Brody.

FOREWORD

IN THE MORE THAN 160 YEARS SINCE *Town & Country*'s inception in 1846, the magazine has covered its readers' private lives and social endeavors. A huge part of both has taken place at home—a location intended not only for carrying out the details of everyday existence, but also for special occasions, entertaining friends, hosting dinner parties, enjoying weekend guests and chaperoning children's sleepovers.

Today, a typical *Town & Country* couple may well have more than one domicile, starting with a private residence in the city or suburbs. They may also own a condominium at a ski resort, a warm-weather retreat, a cottage tucked away in the woods or all of the above (lucky them).

Having multiple homes certainly makes life more complicated and requires a great deal of organization and coordination. But at the same time, it offers a variety of experiences and enables homeowners to expand their design horizons. Furnishings that seem perfectly appropriate for a center-hall Colonial in Connecticut would be wildly out of place in a modern beach house in La Jolla or an A-frame in Aspen. The challenge is to suit the decor to the environment.

Those with confidence in their taste can become their own designers. But if they lack the time and the focus that creating a home requires, they may (and often do) turn to a professional—not just for the architecture and the interior but also for the landscaping. This is usually the case when a project entails building a new house from the ground up. However, such professional help may also be sought for a renovation or an addition to an existing structure. Whatever the case, such efforts require time, money and plenty of patience. Rare is the residence that can be moved into without something being done to it.

Town & Country has published people's homes all over the world over many decades. As times have changed, so has taste—and never more so than in the 1990s and the beginning of the 21st century. We have seen the advent of at-home gyms, offices, fully equipped screening rooms and lavish outdoor entertaining spaces. Computers, flat-screen TVs and other electronic equipment are no longer hidden away, but proudly displayed. Still and all, the effect has to be right to have a place in *Town & Country* and to be included in this, our first book devoted to interior and exterior design.

All of the homes presented—there are thirty—first appeared in the magazine over the past decade and their coverage was assigned (and in some instances written) by Sarah Medford, *T&C*'s director of arts, culture and design, who joined the staff in 1994. Sarah has a keen sense of our readers' taste as well as confidence in her own—two essential qualifications for her position at the magazine and as the editor of this book.

If you've ever dreamed of living the *Town & Country* life, it is within your reach. All you need do is to turn the pages in this book and let us do the rest.

The Montecito home of Herbert and Bui Simon.

Pamela Fiori
EDITOR-AT-LARGE

INTRODUCTION
A PAGE FROM THE GOOD LIFE

I F YOU WERE TO DROP IN ON OUR PLANET RIGHT now from a nearby galaxy, you might conclude that humans are an itinerant people, beloved by our families but driven to spend our lives communicating with them only by cell phone and pager from distant cars, airports, restaurants and city sidewalks. The truth, of course, is quite different. Our home lives have rarely meant more to us. Maybe because the time we spend at home is increasingly valuable, we've become a world of home improvers—builders, renovators, decorators, collectors, online shoppers and magazine clippers. And we long to read stories about others just like us.

When I first came to work as the design editor at *Town & Country* sixteen years ago, I was drawn to its focus on the lives going on inside the houses that filled its pages. You are how you live, I had always thought, and I wanted to explore the connections between housemaking, decorating and personal taste.

This was something the magazine had been doing since its inception in the 1840s. The *Home Journal*, as it was called at the time, was a weekly that had been dreamed up by a dandyish Bostonian, Nathaniel Parker Willis, and a canny New York newspaperman, George Pope Morris, to capture the spirit of the good life in public and in private. Though its name was changed to *Town & Country* in 1901, the periodical's mission, summed up in a quote from Goethe

Terry and Jean de Gunzburg in their Paris kitchen.

at the top of the masthead, remained the same: "We should do the utmost to encourage the beautiful, for the useful encourages itself."

Reporting on the leisure activities of a lucky and occasionally hard-working minority, *Town & Country* quickly found itself covering both sides of Goethe's maxim out of a total identification with its audience (which in turn treated the magazine like a close cousin). In the fall of 1900, for instance, *Town & Country* told its readers about the unhealthful conditions that were leading to typhoid outbreaks in the palatial summer resorts along the East Coast. A few pages later in the same issue, it filled them in on the trend of the season: autumn house parties. "There seems very little disposition to close any of the country houses until after Thanksgiving," the magazine confided in its November edition. "Colonel and Mrs. John Jacob Astor will be at Ferncliff until the middle of December."

At the time I joined *Town & Country*, the magazine was in a profound period of change under the guidance of Pamela Fiori, its new editor in chief. Affluent readers, the audience it had appealed to from its earliest days, were becoming younger, more diverse and more global in the ways they lived. They were traveling more, but also focusing more on family and the home—and *Town & Country* was changing along with them.

Over the past sixteen years, we've explored the relationships between interesting people and the places they call home more intimately than ever before. There are kitchens and bathrooms on our pages now, alongside tales of renovations that would probably have sent Colonel Astor over the edge. There are magical photographs taken on cloudy days; there are casually made beds; and there are rooms filled with flowers where the owner, not the magazine, has chosen to have them. There are chefs, filmmakers, Grammy winners and teachers alongside some latter-day Astors. In getting closer to its subjects, and closer to reality, *Town & Country* continues to speak to its time.

The thirty stories anthologized on the following pages capture the diversity of the stylish subjects we've visited over the past decade—on the town, in the country, and in destinations far away. Each story represents an example of exceptional architecture and design. At the same time, it stands for something equally inspiring: an individual point of view.

"A house is what we design and decorate to suit an image of ourselves, and a home is what we establish by actually living there," Los Angeles decorator and antiques dealer Rose Tarlow told *Town & Country* not long ago, highlighting the critical role personal taste plays in design. Though most of the subjects in this book have collaborated with a professional along the way, they've made sure not to lose themselves in the process. This is an increasingly big challenge, as the economic costs of building and decorating climb, expectations rise along with the budget, and time, the most precious commodity of all, slips away. Many of these stories describe the tricky dance of collaborating with a professional in detail, and there is much to learn from them.

Several projects in the book reflect the latest developments at the forefront of residential architecture and design. Tadao Ando's "Invisible House" for Alessandro Benetton in Italy, for instance, questions the typical relationship between a dwelling and its site, placing the building mostly below grade. Bartholomew Voorsanger's house for Nancy and Dan Brody in Charlottesville, Virginia, uses a geothermal system for heating and cooling and other forms of sustainable technology to guarantee its efficiency in an increasingly energy-conscious world.

Other projects here are delightfully enmeshed in the past. Consider Chatsworth, the ancestral seat of the Dukes of Devonshire for over 400 years. The Derbyshire, England, residence, the largest in the book at 175 rooms, has been renovated, redecorated and annexed as much as any English country house in history, right down into the last decade of the 20th century. Not that you can tell. Chatsworth remains a charismatic distillation of one family and of timeless English country house style. *Town & Country* paid a visit in 1997, and some time ago we received an update from Deborah, the Dowager Duchess of Devonshire.

"I moved eighteen months ago," she wrote. "There are big changes afoot at Chatsworth, instigated by my son and daughter-in-law, so in a sense your piece will be all the more interesting because it fixes the place as it was ten years ago. I thought I should make this quite clear, because it will be a historic, not current, view of the house."

Houses, like people and magazines, are forever on the cusp of change. Which can make books like this one all the more delectable as records of a highly ephemeral art form. Though some of the residents depicted have moved house and moved on in their lives, their histories are still with us in these stories. Some of the lessons here are relevant now; others may suddenly seem more so in the future. Today, thanks to the people who have allowed their homes to become part of our first-ever anthology, *Town & Country* celebrates the good life, in all its variety.

—SARAH MEDFORD
DIRECTOR, *ARTS, CULTURE & DESIGN*

CHAPTER ONE
ON THE
TOWN

T HE DRAMA OF CITY LIFE HAS ALWAYS BEEN A FAVORITE subject at *Town & Country*. We love and admire the grand monuments, the sweeping parks, the towers of power. But when it comes to capturing the creative energy of an urban center like Los Angeles, New York, London or Paris, we prefer to focus not on the places, but on the people who live there, the ones who really make it go.

In the 1930s, the magazine cozied up to debutante Doris Duke on her banquette at New York's El Morocco nightclub. Today we tend to get closer still, visiting actress Mariska Hargitay in her Manhattan duplex, for instance, and hearing about the friends she's made at a nearby firehouse and how the book collection she's building with her husband, actor Peter Hermann, is a microcosm of their relationship.

The couple's library happens to serve as a mini screening room and a party space as well, thanks to their clever decorator, Jeffrey Bilhuber. Such multifunctional rooms are a sign of the times in city dwellings, even among a crowd that can easily afford to have a place for everything and everything in its place. Why? They offer options and flexibility, two must-have features of the urban apartment or town house. And they're simply more interesting to spend time in.

If such hybrid spaces still aren't making their high-living, multitasking home-owners happy, there are two solutions: renovate or move. In a city like New York or London, moving amounts to a full-time preoccupation, not to mention an unscheduled Rorschach test. Just the kind of material that often makes its way onto our pages.

The tour-de-force entryway of Frances Brody's home in Los Angeles.

A MODERN CLASSIC

I T'S A BUSY DAY AT THE GIFT SHOP OF THE HUNtington Library, Art Collections and Botanical Gardens, with hordes of shoppers surveying the books and souvenirs. But the crowd seems to part naturally when Frances Brody approaches the register, five small cardboard kaleidoscopes balanced in her hands. She pays for them and is soon on her way to rejoin her friends. "Weren't you getting coffee?" asks one, as Brody pulls a toy from her bag and holds it up to the light. "I just love these," she remarks, brushing off the question in order to complete her thought. "Take a look. I want to send one to my granddaughter—they're so much fun."

Fun is something Frances Brody seems to generate. She is at once irrepressible and generous—able, as if by twisting some internal kaleidoscope, to influence events in colorful and felicitous ways. Twice a mother, twice a grandmother, she has also created a great art collection and a remarkable house. Her life has glittered with Hollywood dinner parties, portrait sittings with Cecil Beaton, long summers in Saint-Jean-Cap-Ferrat, studio visits with Matisse.

"Francie has certainly 'been there, seen that'—she has led a life of extraordinary privilege," says her longtime friend Robert Ritchie, the Huntington's director of research. "But she would absolutely never use her worldliness to put you down. Her scope of reference just happens to be extremely broad."

OVERLEAF: A spirit of opulence and refinement characterizes Brody's vast living room, which has three conversation areas and a plant-filled atrium behind glass.

RIGHT: A female figure beckons from the garden beyond the dining room.

Right now Brody's interests are focused specifically on the Huntington, the former estate of railroad baron Henry Huntington, which opened to the public in 1928. This has meant regular trips back and forth between her house on the west side of Los Angeles and the institution's headquarters in the San Gabriel Valley. The Huntington has undertaken several major projects; Brody, an overseer, is heavily involved. (This may not sound like a kick to everyone, but Francie, as all her friends call her, is not everyone. Inviting a visitor to join her on an extended Huntington tour, she sets the tone: "It will be a day of hooky and fun, as far as I'm concerned.")

Brody leads her friends through the gardens—the cherry allée, with its vista of the snow-topped San Gabriel Mountains, evokes a Japanese print—to the new greenhouses. A tall and slender woman, she wears gold earrings, a red turtleneck, gray flannel trousers and white tennis sneakers for navigating the areas still under construction. Her bearing is confident, her face animated—especially when she's expressing one of her forthright opinions. "I'm feeling very sorry for the art at the Huntington right now," she says matter-of-factly. "It often falls behind the gardens and the library, both of which were part of the original estate. And the art galleries desperately need work." On visiting the newly reinstalled fine-and-decorative-arts building, she remarks to a young

and serious curator making the rounds with her, "It needs porcelain and flowers. I mean porcelain out in the open—not in cases. If the Getty can live dangerously, so can we."

"Francie is an original, and there just aren't that many original women around in this town anymore," says Terry Stanfill, a friend of more than thirty years. "For one thing, she has strong, vocal opinions. For another, she has an unsparing sense of style, which she's stuck with for as long as I've known her. Francie is simply a constant." Her favorite couturier, James Galanos, now retired, puts it this way: "Francie has wonderful style. She's always had a very sure idea of how she wanted to look. And she has never deviated from that."

The prime example of Brody's uncompromising taste is her house, an essay in modernist glamour completed in 1950. Brody and her late husband, Sidney, a businessman, commissioned the four-bedroom house when they were still in their early thirties, a young couple with two children, new to California. Since then, almost nothing has been altered. Books have accumulated on the shelves, paintings have migrated from room to room, some of the upholstery has been redone, but that's it. And yet the house is no time capsule. It looks as fresh now as it must have in the early fifties, when the Brodys began to play a role in the social and cultural lives of Los Angeles.

Architect A. Quincy Jones angled the Brody house on its site to maximize light and views in the major rooms, all of which open onto terraces.

"We had so much fun doing our house," says Brody, sitting in a plushly upholstered armchair in her living room. "That's very unusual, you know. Building a house is supposed to be torture. But we'd lived in quite a few before this one, and we finally hit on two men who were good enough to put up with all our clippings and ideas. Billy Haines, the interior designer, and Quincy Jones, the architect, both respected us. We had a wonderful relationship—we took a year to plan, a year to build, and a case of whiskey a week."

The house now deserves a glass of Champagne. Terribly stylish in 1950, today it epitomizes L.A.'s look of the moment in its synthesis of two design movements currently back in fashion: California midcentury modernist architecture and elegant, Hollywood Moderne decor. Among the young princes of film and fashion there is no hotter acquisition right now than a flat-roofed, steel-framed house sheathed in glass. (Tom Ford didn't start the trend, but he recently entered at the top when he bought a 1955 Bel Air house designed by Richard Neutra.) Realtors, hunting for pedigreed properties to meet the demand, are scaling unfamiliar driveways across the L.A. basin in search of overlooked work by the so-called "Case Study" architects (Quincy Jones was one), who created model homes for *Arts & Architecture* magazine from 1945 to 1962. And while many buyers want to retrofit these austere light boxes with fifties-era

with a more informal California lifestyle," Hines observes. "It's just a wonderful merger of client, designers, time and place."

"When I look back at my phone book from that period, I can't believe the preponderance of movie people in it," says Brody, sipping black coffee from a vermeil cup, a slice of buttered and toasted pound cake on a plate beside her. "But L.A. life was very ghettoized when we arrived. We had the most eclectic group of friends of anyone I knew. Sid was in the aviation and real estate businesses, so we knew those people. We certainly knew the movie people; they were our chums. Joan Crawford and the Gary Coopers were friends, and Jack and Mary Benny lived right behind us. And we also knew the social people. It was a cross-section of town.

"I remember trying to get some attention for the new UCLA Arts Council," she continues. "They'd mounted a wonderful Picasso exhibit, and I was organizing an opening, which was a new idea for that museum. We had it at Romanoff's—everybody came," she recalls, her eyes sparkling. "I remember Rocky Cooper, Gary's wife, said to me, 'How did you do it?' And I borrowed a favorite line of my husband's: 'Stick with me, baby, and you'll find diamonds in your suitcase.'"

With Francie Brody, that's almost the way it was. She had grown up outside Chicago, the third child of Albert and Flora Lasker. Her father

George Nelson sofas and Eames recliners, a growing number of people are seeking out the infinitely more luxurious, high-style furniture of that time, especially "cocktail modern" pieces custom-designed for Hollywood projects by Billy Haines and his contemporaries.

Examples of such decor, including burnished, leather-topped desks, an ebony dining table that seats thirty and tuffetlike "conversation stools" designed to swivel 360 degrees, lend the Brody house a spirit of opulence and refinement that perfectly suits the prosperous nineties. That spirit was very much of its time, too, says UCLA professor of history and architecture Thomas Hines. "The Brody house expresses postwar optimism, the urge to live well again, and certainly the ideal of mixing beautiful forms

A tabletop-sized Henry Moore bronze.

was a pioneering figure in advertising and marketing, responsible for the launches of products from Kleenex to Lucky Strikes to Sunkist orange juice. His ideas made him rich, and in later life he became a well-known arts patron (as did his third wife and widow, Mary). He was also extremely well connected. As a result, Brody recalls, "We were always surrounded by people from sports, radio and theater because of my father's work. I was very lucky in that way."

What can't be explained so easily is the sureness of her taste. The house, on a 480-acre estate near Lake Forest, Illinois, was designed in the French Provincial style by Chicago architect David Adler, and decorated by Adler's sister, the esteemed interior designer Frances Elkins. That's a long way from Hollywood modernism.

On the other hand, Mill Road Farm, as they called it, had real style. Its greenhouses were full of Belgian grapes; the family could stroll among six miles of clipped hedges or play on the private golf course. And that kind of luxe, once experienced, tends to reappear. Brody, moreover, was exposed to tastemakers, starting with her parents. "Samuel Marx, the interior designer and architect, was a family friend," she says. "He was devilishly attractive, *méchant*, and a born flirt. He built a perfectly beautiful house for some friends of ours, and together we went to a party there when I was a teenager. Later I asked him why it didn't feel right to me. 'You know,' he said, 'a house is only as good as its owners.'"

How would Brody make use of all that she'd absorbed? "When Sid and I first came to L.A., in 1948, we rented a house to see where we wanted to live," she remembers, the coffee now gone and the pound cake still untouched. "It was in Beverly Hills, on 'the flats.' They're really high-class tenements, you know—you had a pool on either side of you, with fences between. In the summer, when the phone rang, you didn't know if it was yours or somebody else's."

Unable to find a house she loved after seeing some 125, Francie told Sid that they would have to build. "We didn't have an architect in mind, so we started with the interior designer," she says, explaining an approach that is much more common now than it was then. The Brodys learned about Haines through Bill and Edie Goetz; Bill was one of the founders of 20th Century Fox, Edie the daughter of Louis B. Mayer and a popular Hollywood hostess. When the Brodys finally met Haines at a dinner party at Joan Crawford's, they were ready to hire him.

Together they began the search for an architect. Haines had done a great deal of work with the traditionalists around town, including Paul Williams and James Dolena. But the Brodys wanted a modern house. "We didn't want Neutra, because of his floor plans—you always had to walk through the living room to get to the kitchen, and that just wasn't the way we lived," Brody explains. "We ended up hiring Quincy Jones."

The design team was a gamble, to say the least. Jones was a young, Missouri-born modernist with no brilliant houses on his record. Haines was a silent-screen actor turned decorator to the stars. While Jones had spent the years leading up to the Brody commission designing tract houses on minuscule lots, Haines had been perfecting an exceedingly swank traditionalism in houses for George Cukor, Carole Lombard, and Jack and Ann Warner, among others. By 1946, he'd begun experimenting with modernism. The Brody commission brought the men together for the first time. So fruitful was the match, the pair went on to do seven more houses together, including the Bel Air home of Betsy and Alfred Bloomingdale, and Sunnylands, the Palm Springs estate of Lee and Walter Annenberg.

Focusing the designers' talents was the Brodys' enlightened point of view. "Sid and I had learned through experience that if you had two public rooms downstairs, people always gravitated to the smaller one," says Brody. "So we decided to avoid that by having just one big living room downstairs, and we put the study upstairs, near our bedroom. The dining room came off the gallery, and the children had their own wing." The kitchen and pantry, off the dining room, were also accessible through doors to the garage—so no one ever saw groceries, or the people who would unpack them, going through the living room. Jones had bested Neutra, as far as the Brodys were concerned.

When it came time to discuss the specifics of the decor, Brody recalls, "Bill told us, 'Now we have to talk about color. Are there any colors you don't like?' 'Brown,' said Sid. Bill looked him up and down. Sid was wearing a brown sweater, beige shirt, tan slacks and cordovan shoes. Bill replied, 'Sid, that must be the nicest navy blue ensemble you've got on that I've ever seen.' And so we did a lot with brown."

The Brodys' West Side neighbors must have been bemused, to say the least, when construction was completed in late 1950. In a community of sedate European knockoffs, the house was unique, a low, pristinely white brick building that angled itself across the lot as though it were sunbathing. (Today it's Brody's turn to be horrified by her neighbors, as they top off their neo-Georgian "manors" with balustrades of foam.) In one place the house grew a terraced second story; in others it sported springboard-style roof overhangs. The outside was less extraordinary, however, than the inside, where draperies were on push buttons, plants watered themselves via a built-in sprinkler system, and lights were preset to different "moods," a feature only now becoming affordable some fifty years later.

Eventually the glamorous modern decor passed out of style. But Brody never considered redecorating: she knew what she liked, and this was it. The house continues to delight her today. She experiments in the garden, reads a great deal, hosts the occasional party and welcomes her children and grandchildren on their visits from the East Coast. Several times a year she goes to see them, which also gives her a chance to catch up on area museum shows.

Art is her abiding interest. "Frankly, I don't know what I'd do without it," she says. Both Brody and her husband were active collectors who confidently bought works by Picasso, Braque, Matisse, Miró, Giacometti, Modigliani and Degas while they were underappreciated. Though she sold most of her collection years ago, Brody still has a few favorites, including a ceramic-tile wall mural by Matisse that measures just over twelve by eleven feet. *La Gerbe* (1953) is one of only a few such murals the artist ever made, and it fills an entire wall of Brody's open-air courtyard with jubilant, dancing leaves.

The story of the mural is one that many of Brody's friends consider "classic Francie." In 1953, she and her husband visited Matisse at his home in the Hôtel Régina just outside Nice to see his maquette for the planned piece. Neither of them felt it worked; a long silence ensued, and after the meeting they had the uncomfortable task of telling him that they would prefer something different. He told the couple to return the next day, and when they did they found the artist willing to create a new piece for them.

"Only Francie could tell Henri Matisse to try again," laughs Robert Ritchie.

In his book *Matisse: Father and Son*, John Russell includes a letter from the artist to his son, the New York dealer Pierre Matisse, that takes the story one step further. Of the Brodys' second visit the elder Matisse wrote, "Their whole manner had been transformed since the previous day. They could not have been warmer, and seemed ready to take anything that I chose for them. They did say that they would like something

With midcentury modernism all the rage in Los Angeles, Frances Brody seems a seer for holding on to her house and its original decor.

quite simple—a vivid scatter of color on a white background. The price was not discussed." In other words, not only did the Brodys actually tell Matisse to try again, but they also told him just what they wanted the second time around.

Years ago, Brody gave Matisse's maquette for the mural to the UCLA Hammer Museum. She has long supported Los Angeles cultural institutions, notably the Huntington, UCLA and the L.A. County Museum of Art. But she is very clear about the nature of her involvement.

"I hate the word 'philanthropy,'" she says, tensing as if the syllables themselves were slithering around her neck. "It sounds pretentious—I wish I had enough money to be a philanthropist. I'm a participant. It gives me great pleasure." She gives of herself, especially to the Huntington, an institution she insists has been terribly misunderstood. "Everyone has always thought the Huntington was very rich because Mr. Huntington left it a generous endowment," Brody remarks as she pilots her caramel-colored Lexus back over the hills a few days later for another meeting in San Marino. "But the effects of the stock market crash in the early thirties left it hugely reduced. And now, in raising capital, we have to battle the preconceived public notion that the museum has money and so doesn't need more."

Brody hopes a temporary exhibitions building will bring a fresh constituency to the Huntington just as the ever-expanding botanical gardens have. And if it doesn't, she'll doubtless be on the phone with a few new suggestions.

"You know, I don't say whatever I want just to be different," she remarks, maneuvering her car across four lanes of traffic on the Hollywood Freeway. "Being older is rather interesting. As you age, everything jells and comes together, and it gets more fascinating. I have new ideas about so many things. You have to speak up."

"I've lived through so much," she adds after a long pause. "I've been very lucky. When I was fourteen, I had bushy black hair and I said to myself, 'Well, you're not going to be any beauty, so you'd better just be yourself and have a good time.' And I did." She still does.

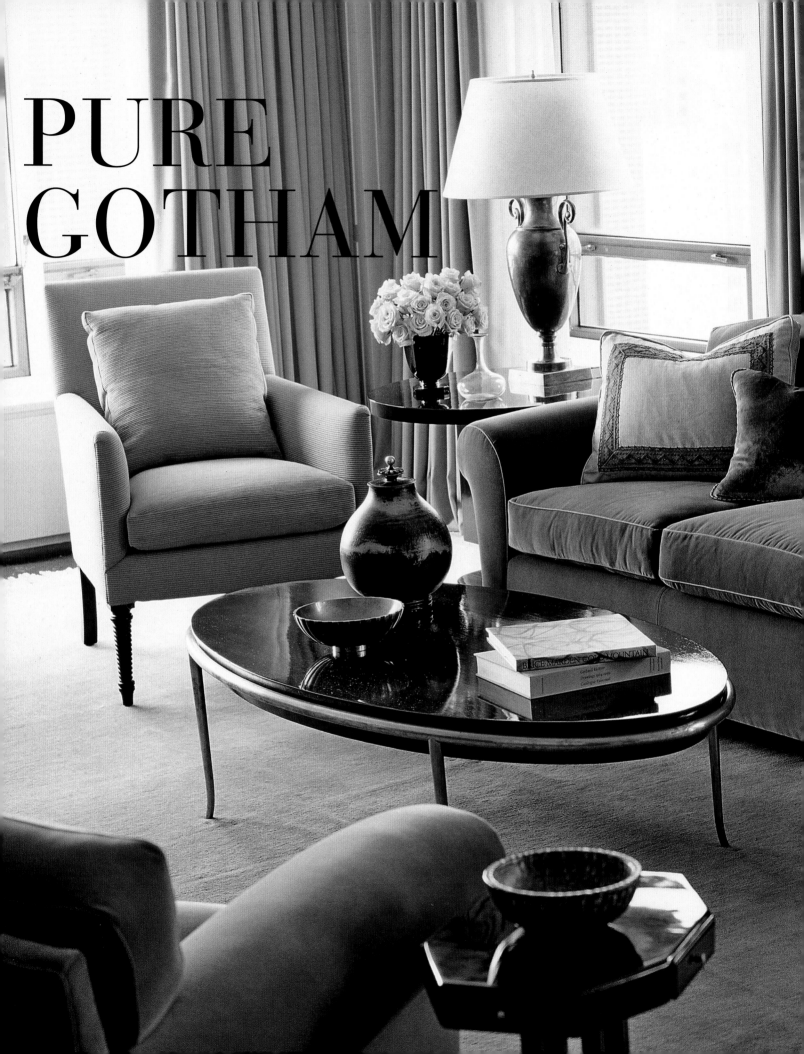

PURE
GOTHAM

OVERLEAF: Caroline Hirsch's New York living room features a custom sofa covered in velvet; the armchairs to either side are from Holly Hunt.

RIGHT: An avid buyer of 20th-century art and design, Hirsch lives with a 1955 painting by Joan Mitchell over the living-room mantel and early-to-midcentury French and Scandinavian ceramics.

T HOUGH CAROLINE HIRSCH IS THE REIGN-ing queen of American comedy clubs, the undisputed doyenne of laugh-out-loud delight, the physical realm over which she rules—more often than not dressed in head-to-toe Prada, head-to-toe Dior or head-to-toe Tom Ford for YSL Rive Gauche—is decidedly more dungeon than castle. In fact, Carolines on Broadway should actually be called Carolines Under Broadway, because all 11,000 square feet of the "Cadillac of comedy clubs" (as *Variety* very excitedly anointed it) are burrowed beneath the brittle gray concrete of Manhattan's Great White Way. It's not unlike a bunker, albeit a bunker with a jaunty theatrical decor that references such iconic comedic motifs as harlequins, pantomime and jokers in the service of an idiosyncratic school of design that the club's architect, Paul Haigh, enjoys labeling "neomedievalism."

And though Hirsch never complains about the inordinate amount of time she spends squirreled away there, it is telling that, at the end of each workday, when she leaves her subterranean lair in Times Square, she heads, like some fading phototropic plant, directly for the light.

In other words, it's probably no accident that Hirsch's Mercedes is a convertible. Just as it's probably no accident that the Shingle-style weekend retreat she and her partner, Andrew Fox,

LEFT: In the dining room, 1930s Jules Leleu chairs circle a table custom-designed by Glenn Gissler; the painting is Ross Bleckner's 2001 *Flow and Return*.

RIGHT: A curving bronze torso by Auguste Rodin echoes the serpentine staircase in the foyer.

a lawyer, built in the Hamptons has conspicuously overscale windows and a luminous master bedroom located on the third floor of the 9,000-square-foot house perched, no surprise, atop the tallest dune on a site overlooking both Mecox Bay and the Atlantic Ocean.

And then there's Hirsch's new Manhattan apartment, which is situated nine neat blocks due east of her club. The leisurely crosstown stroll takes about twenty minutes, door to door, factoring in the time necessary for the elevator in the thirty-eight-story building to rocket thirty-five floors straight up to a 4,000-square-foot duplex with views that would make Icarus swoon.

The apartment is in one of the two monumental towers that architect Wallace Harrison completed in 1966 on a plot wedged between the brave-new-world grandeur of the United Nations complex and the old-world gentility of Beekman Place. Hirsch had already spent some seventeen years in a duplex in the west building before she, Fox and Emma, the duo's bearded collie, moved to a slightly larger one in the east. "I was going to redecorate my old apartment, and then this came on the market, and I wanted a little more space," says Hirsch, who confesses that, in addition to the two extra rooms, she wanted to make a fresh stylistic start. So she managed to convince herself that, as she says, "Maybe it would be easier to buy this apartment than to redo the one I was in."

Encouraging Hirsch to make the leap from west tower to east was Glenn Gissler, the Rhode Island School of Design–trained, Manhattan-based designer who had worked with her on her Hamptons house. She initially asked him to consider redesigning her duplex, but he demurred. And understandably so: the apartment was head-to-toe Art Deco. Think Ruhlmann, Dunand, Leleu. Think Mr. Chow's on East 57th Street.

"I said, 'Just sell it and move. It would be easier,'" Gissler recalls advising Hirsch. Which she happily did, never mind that the matter of "easier" didn't quite ring true in the end. As for why she didn't consider trying another location in Manhattan, say, Park or Fifth avenues, she reports, "It's hard to leave this kind of light. It's very, very different. And the view . . ."

Style modernism. This is partly because they were originally conceived as office blocks; when the commercial-real-estate market faltered during their construction, the developers decided to reconfigure them as apartments and chose to go with the eminently bankable Park Avenue mold.

"The walls are of glass, but the space is not modern," says Gissler. "It's carved up into more traditional rooms."

In other words, the apartment's aluminum-and-glass curtain wall said one thing, while its floor plan—public rooms and kitchen on the first level, four bedrooms on the second—said something else altogether. Which was fine with Hirsch and Gissler, although the absence of any semblance of texture or ornamentation or material richness was not. So they added them.

"It was really like a blank canvas," recalls Hirsch. "White walls, no moldings."

"It was a lot of work," Gissler reports.

And this address is famously inhospitable to contractors and apartment owners who are intent on doing a lot of work.

"The rules for renovations are extreme," says Gissler. "You have a maximum of twelve weeks a year, and in those twelve weeks you get only five of what they call 'noise days.' It's probably the most difficult complex to work with in New York City." So Gissler had as much of the project fabricated outside the apartment as

Virtually untouched since the 1960s, Hirsch's second apartment was a kind of time capsule of the period in which it was built—complete with lime-green shag carpeting in the service hall, a graphic (and glossy) black-and-white palette and one of those open-tread cantilevered staircases that were considered glamorous back in the days when Truman Capote and Johnny and Joanna Carson called the buildings home. (Today the residents include Walter Cronkite, Dina Merrill and photographer Gordon Parks.)

Though the two Harrison towers rising over the East River have been likened to 860–880 Lake Shore Drive, Chicago's twin residential buildings designed by Mies van der Rohe and completed in 1951, they have neither an unimpeachable provenance nor anything approaching the same rigorous commitment to International

Not even Emma, the bearded collie, can resist the kitchen's view of the U.N., even on a cloudy day.

possible. When nothing more could be done, the wham-bam twelve-week installation began.

As the designer tells it, his initial strategy for the renovation was established by looking at a certain Picasso painting, which offered, to his eye, "a kind of architectural clarity, plus a warm, rich palette—modern but not cold." He also understood from the get-go that the rooms needed to have "more clarity in terms of their relationship to the mullion grid of the building." Which they did not have.

Toward that end, he and his senior designer, John Kureck, had the interior walls and partitions shifted, moved and realigned while maintaining the basic layout. They then introduced eight-foot mahogany doors with thick complementary frames and custom-designed nickel hardware, all of which seem solid to both the eye and the hand. "A huge amount of the apartment was custom built to very detailed plans, over a substantial period of time," adds Gissler. "None of the architectural details were ordered from stock."

Both Hirsch and Gissler were determined to include, rather than compete with, what some might call the rhapsody-in-blue view. And so they opted for an interior in a muted palette that shifts from white to cream to ivory to beige to taupe to brown to various shades of blue without ever once lurching,

then chose quiet, mainly 20th-century furniture in subtle finishes and second-touch materials that form a foil not only for the view but also for the ambitious art collection that Hirsch has been assembling for the duplex. Gissler understood that the art was to occupy pride of visual place in the dreamy series of luxe, low-decibel rooms he conceived.

"The apartment feels grounded," he says. "Despite being on the thirty-fifth and thirty-sixth floors, it doesn't have that kind of uneasy, floaty high-rise feeling." The result, he says, is worth the almost-two-year endeavor.

"One thing about working with Caroline is that she has an incredible commitment to completion," says Gissler. "She sees it through down to the last detail."

And it's true. From the Picasso etching in the entryway to the Pratesi linens in the powder room, Hirsch's duplex is, as architects like to say, d-o-n-e done.

"A lot of clients get tired, or they run out of enthusiasm or money or something," continues Gissler, who, when asked if there were any financial constraints on the project, says, "You can't really call Caroline's budget modest, not by most people's circumstances. But the sky was not the limit."

Perhaps he's right. Perhaps the sky was not the limit. On the other hand, it was the idea.

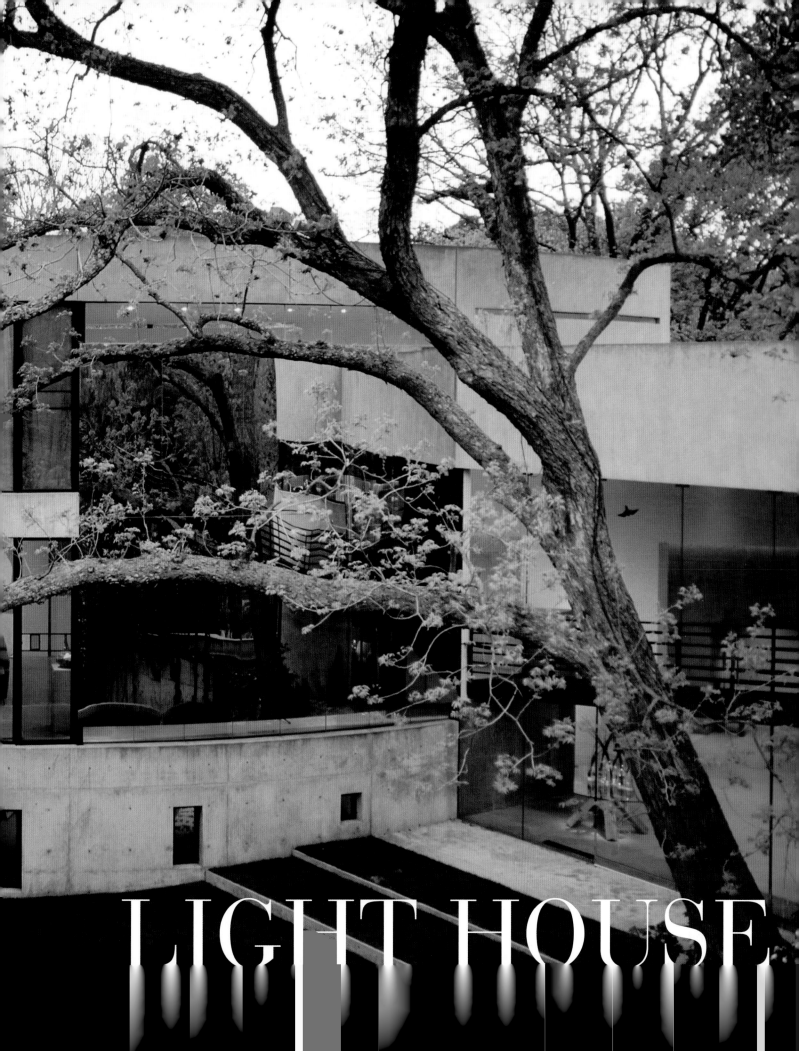

LIGHT HOUSE

OVERLEAF: The Rose house, designed by Antoine Predock, occupies a sylvan setting along Dallas's Turtle Creek.

RIGHT: An American 1930s sofa, an Ernest Boiçeau carpet and sculpture by Richard Tuttle populate an alcove off the living room.

U NLESS YOU KNOW WHAT YOU'RE LOOK-ing for, Deedie and Rusty Rose's house is almost invisible from the street. Its windowless facade of ragged limestone blocks is easy to mistake for a waterfront bulkhead along Turtle Creek, which runs behind the property, or maybe an overgrown quarry (the Roses have probably heard far more unflattering comparisons from their neighbors over the years). The cavelike entrance sets up an expec-tation of darkness within; instead the house dematerializes as you enter, leaving the impression that you've simply passed through a garden wall and are standing on a light-dappled lawn shaded by the prettiest pecan tree in Dallas. It's a confounding experience—is there a house here at all?

Certainly not one as the city had imagined it before 1993, when the Roses moved in. Their neighborhood, Highland Park, one of the oldest in the city, is a catalogue of traditional styles whose Norman and Georgian pages are particularly dog-eared. In com-missioning architectural seeker Antoine Predock to build them a manor house for the 21st century, the Roses introduced a cool cat among the canines, a languid gray eminence that, without so much as raising its head above the trees, has effectively dispatched with the pretensions of prevailing Dallas architecture.

This wasn't exactly the couple's goal. Committed simply to

A polished steel panel mounted on the rear of the house reflects a lyrical pecan tree.

creating a house for themselves that was firmly of its time and place, the Roses, long-standing and influential patrons of the arts, interviewed five architects before settling on the Albuquerque-based Predock. "I wanted to find a brain that showed me it was looking in new ways," recalls Deedie Rose of her initial meetings with the five candidates. "That kind of creativity is what will ultimately have the most impact on others. And it has been fascinating. Now I never want to be without a project.

"When I went to see Antoine, I knew almost immediately he was it: he seemed deeply connected to the land and the culture," she says, referring not to Highland Park's manicured flower beds and multiple bridge nights, but to her southwestern city's geological roots and the complexities of modern life there. Often tagged a poet and a visionary for his nature-based formal explorations, Predock has designed transcendent buildings for private clients as well as for cultural institutions throughout the U.S. and abroad. By now the Rose residence has become a local icon, and with good reason—it has subverted expectations about what contemporary residential architecture feels like to live in.

Above all, the house has great warmth and elegance. Once your eyes adjust to the light indoors, you begin to notice the limestone floor—a soft, powdery gray—and the white ceiling

In the living room, designer Emily Summers made restrained choices in deference to the dramatic creekside view. The armchairs on the left are by Michel Roux-Spitz; the daybed is by artist Rosemarie Trockel and the sofa in the foreground by couturier Charles James.

that forms an arc some twenty feet above. The dappled lawn is just behind a glass wall straight ahead, and stone steps to the right lead up to an expansive living room and library. From here the house unfolds like a sublime version of an Escher drawing, all angles, steps and half floors. Arrayed over six levels are a kitchen at entry height; a dining room in a circular tower above; two guest rooms a half-flight down on the ground floor; a living room and a library on the mezzanine level; a master suite and a private terrace for bird watching atop the library; and a roof terrace. Though it amounts to 10,000 square feet, the house never feels unnecessarily large, and the Roses use all of it when they entertain or have their two grown children and their families to visit. Will, a managing director of a hedge fund, lives not far away in Dallas; Lela, a fashion designer, lives in Manhattan.

Given the toughness of its materials—concrete, limestone, steel and glass—the house might have gone in a much chillier direction if it hadn't been for the diversity of Deedie's tastes and the decisive input of Emily Summers. As the interior designer of choice for much of the Dallas elite, Emily is adept at giving people what they want. But it's clear that her heart starts to race a lot faster when she gets to collaborate with an architect on a contemporary project like the Rose house. (Over the years her design team has also

OVERLEAF: The moods of the house progress from museumlike grandeur in the entry hall, where a Sol LeWitt drawing fills the staircase wall, to hushed seclusion in the dining tower to the right at the top of the stairs.

LEFT: The library is the site of frequent meetings between Emily Summers (left) and Deedie Rose.

included Mil Bodron and Kimberly Barrett.) The furnishings and their arrangement reflect the creative journey Deedie and Emily have taken since the late '80s, before the house was finished, and continue to make, because pieces still come and go. The living room is indicative: there are new plush silk carpets over the polished concrete floors; a Swedish silver tea set from the 1930s sits beside a Richard Tuttle sculpture; and a pair of ivory-colored sofas designed by the couturier Charles James forms a crescent facing the view.

"It was a constant learning process, and it still is," says Deedie. "Emily and I have traveled to New York, Paris, Milan, Tokyo, endlessly and tirelessly, looking and buying. She is amazing with her resources. She's always digging up new things, and she always has options. I would fall in love with something, and she'd say to me, 'We can't buy anything unless we can find at least two places to put it.' We were always pulling out the floor plan—I had to learn from that."

"Deedie didn't want a furniture museum," Emily says, "and early on there were some prototype pieces that didn't fare too well here. But we moved beyond them into a real juxtaposition of hard and soft; simple older furniture with new pieces. I think that's given the house a soul.

"I'm a modernist who loves clean lines," she continues, "but I also love the expressive nature of the decorative arts. And the emotional resonance of these pieces in combination with Deedie and Rusty's art is so powerful." The couple's collection includes work by some of the art world's most revered members, among them Tuttle Gerhard Richter, Louise Bourgeois, Robert Ryman and Sol LeWitt, alongside pieces by rising and midcareer artists like Wolfgang Laib, Brad Tucker and Anne Chu.

Back in the late 1970s, when Deedie and Emily first met as docents at the Dallas Museum of Art, their conversations about their work would carry over onto the bleachers of their sons' sporting events and out into the dark streets of Highland Park after dinner parties. It was hard to stop talking, and it still is.

"Deedie and I have the same stamina," says Emily. "It's always one last gallery, one last store, one last meal. She'll come to the opera with me, and I'll go to the theater with her. I think she's always too busy; she thinks I'm always too busy. And we appreciate the same things—we have many of the same 'aha' moments."

This often happens at galleries and art fairs, where the friends share a history of splurging. "Do I buy?" Deedie asks with a sigh, her soft gray eyes sparkling. Deedie may share Emily's drive, but she wears it under a mantle of deceptive calm. "Yes, I'm the consummate shopper," she admits. "I've bought things I really love." One of those things, a chrome-yellow painting by Pop artist Alex Hay, hangs in the hallway just outside Deedie's kitchen door. Emily has already pointed it out as an example of "one of the ones that got away," pieces both women fell for but Deedie ended up bringing home. Emily always gets a consolation prize, however: she has a hand in deciding where it goes.

In 2005, the two cochaired Dallas's charity auction Two by Two for AIDS and Art, which their friends Howard and Cindy Rachofsky hosted. The event, which benefited amfAR (the American Foundation for AIDS Research) and the Dallas Museum of Art, was preceded by a week's worth of parties, including one held by Deedie and Rusty at their home. Such evenings have always been on the couple's calendar.

"The minute this house was finished, Deedie opened it up for civic events and showed people how you can live with great architecture," Emily says. "It was really a galvanizing experience for the city. And since then a lot of first-rate buildings have gone up in Dallas. Steven Holl, Richard Meier and many others have designed houses here."

Though Deedie is far too modest to suggest that she and Rusty have played a role in Dallas's architectural flowering, she does admit to having invited her entire neighborhood in for a look when the house was complete. After six years of design and construction and results that

resembled nothing else in town, she knew it was the right thing to do. By this time, and despite her continued tinkering, she's grown used to the constant flow of students and collectors who want to see how she and Rusty have made a home for art within something very close to an art piece itself.

The dining tower at dusk. The circular room within, a favorite place for the Roses to host dinner parties, adjoins a roof terrace surrounded by mature trees.

A HAVEN IN PARIS

I LOVE THE PROVINCIAL AIR OF THIS NEIGHBOR-hood," says Terry de Gunzburg with infectious enthusiasm as she describes her corner of Paris—the sixteenth arrondissement's southern part, still known as Auteuil. "One goes everywhere on foot—to great schools, marvelous shops and open markets. We have the quality of city life and the pleasures of the country because we are surrounded by gardens, parks and the Bois de Boulogne."

Terry, a cosmetics designer, and her husband, Jean, a scientist, also happen to own what many people consider to be the most captivating house in the area: it was designed in 1891 by Art Nouveau visionary Hector-Germain Guimard at the tender age of twenty-four. With the help of Jacques Grange, their good friend and decorator, the de Gunzburgs have filled it with an eclectic hit parade of 20th-century art and design, reflecting their shared love of color, craftsmanship and wit.

Today Terry's color sense is demonstrated in a vivid peony-rose and orchid-pink shirt, teamed with cyclamen silk pants and a black sweater, her dark hair framing a glowing complexion and a flash of raspberry lip gloss. We're sipping coffee in the sitting room; before us is a 1950s Jean Royère table, where small pots pop with violet- and lavender-colored sweet peas. The countrified posies are local, from Monsieur Froment—"he is a poet of flowers"—whose

boutique is only a hop, skip and a jump away on the Rue d'Auteuil.

The de Gunzburgs' story is local, too, a bona fide neighborhood romance. In 1993 Terry was working as creative director of Yves Saint Laurent Cosmetics, dreaming up such makeup innovations as Touche d'Éclat, the reflective concealer that is still a YSL best seller. Jean, the soft-spoken possessor of an irresistible smile, was heading a team of cancer researchers at the Institut Curie. Both were divorced and living in the area, and their daughters (Terry's Marion and Éloise, Jean's Noémie, Clara and Géraldine) were teenaged school friends. "After a year and a half of seeing each other on the school steps, at parents' meetings and at children's birthday parties, he invited me to dinner," Terry reminisces. "Between the leeks vinaigrette and the crème brûlée, we had a reciprocal *coup de foudre*. We haven't been apart since."

With five children to accommodate (it's now up to seven, with the addition of sons Samuel and Eytan), the two-bedroom Guimard house shouldn't even have been on their radar. But on a chance drive past, Terry glimpsed its ocher bricks peeping from behind "amazing hundred-year-old wisteria" that provoked a return visit with Jean. "Walking in through the facade, with its mosaics and stained-glass windows, felt like walking into a fairy tale," she remembers.

"We said, 'Okay, we'll live squashed together.' We were both conquered by its charm."

They bought the house in 1994 and then called on the prodigious expertise of Grange, who had already collaborated separately with both de Gunzburgs—on the Saint Laurent Institute with Terry and on previous apartment with Jean. (Grange's early mentor, the legendary Henri Samuel, had also worked with Jean's late mother, Minda Bronfman, on the family *hôtel particulier* in Paris.) Given the couple's close friendship with the designer on a weekend with him in St. Rémy, they bought the Provençal house he subsequently decorated for them, it's not surprising that their partnership has resulted in exceptional, utterly enchanting interiors. Grange restructured the interior layout, creating four new bedrooms to make six in all and renovating the ground floor into two large rooms and an entryway.

"The house was a Hector Guimard folly, but inside it was pure '70s," Grange recalls. "The only trace of the original was a staircase and a few stained-glass windows. I thought that the way to make it true to itself again was to rework the poetry of the place on an Art Nouveau theme—not making an homage, but developing it as a fantasy with a Guimard touch. We played with Jean and Terry's collections, their taste and the simplicity of the house."

OVERLEAF: Zaha Hadid's red divan (far left) shares the family room with Jean Royère's 1940s sofa and chairs.

LEFT: The couple often entertains in the kitchen, with its harlequin tile floor chosen by Terry.

RIGHT: In the living room, a quartet of Christian Bérard gouaches, circa 1945, hang above a Jean Royère table.

Gustave Serrurier-Bovy; a striking space with an open fireplace, it's especially popular for the couple's winter dinner parties. The ravishing master-bedroom suite, which includes twin dressing rooms and studies, is designed "like a secret box," says Grange, whose plan drew on the paneled rooms of Jean-Michel Frank as well as elements of Asian architecture. Sycamore floors, walls of leather in one room and of straw marquetry in another and Japanese-style bamboo blinds, or *sudares*, at the windows bring a honeyed light to the suite even on cloudy days.

Furniture, found half by decorator and half by clients, is as practical as it is alluring. The pieces include a stunning 1940s André Groult cabinet of ivory and macassar ebony in the dining room and, in the family room, Jean Royère's Ours Polaire armchairs from the same decade and Zaha Hadid's contemporary sweeping divan (it doubles as the boys' trampoline). Grange pulled a rabbit out of a hat when he discovered an original Guimard ceramic mantelpiece in New York that flawlessly fit the fireplace in the living room.

"Jacques understands the personality of the people he works for," maintains Jean de Gunzburg, who was involved in every decision and choice of object. "We had a dialogue, not that we always agreed. I hate 'decoration' things like mirrors. Walls are for paintings."

In 1999, when the fifties-era town house next door became available, the couple leaped at the chance to buy it and join the two buildings for more space (they already shared a common wall). Grange seamlessly linked the two residences by reorienting the Guimard staircase and converting part of the town house's terrace into an enclosed winter garden. The result is a capacious house measuring more than 10,000 square feet, with eight bedrooms and eight baths spread over three floors.

The de Gunzburgs' interiors have been conceived to delight, not by proclaiming their dazzling opulence but by whispering polished perfection. On the ground floor, a large kitchen and dining area was inspired by the Arts-and-Crafts style of Guimard's Belgian contemporary

In the master bath, floors and walls are of sycamore or straw marquetry; window shades are Japanese bamboo *sudares* trimmed by Lilou Marquand.

Underlining his thesis is an overflow of pictures awaiting placement. The collection, ranging from Picasso to Bérard to Bacon, has become Terry's major source of inspiration for By Terry, the cosmetics line she founded in 1998, before leaving Saint Laurent. "I adore the orange backgrounds and mixed pinks of Bacon, the color accords of Matisse," she says. "At Saint Laurent, I entered into the religion of color of a master. Now I might retranslate the atmosphere and palette of Paul Klee into a cosmetics collection."

As a child, Terry had a novel introduction to cosmetics. Her father was a research pharmacist, and "when other families made cakes with their mothers on Sundays, we blended eaux de cologne from essential oils and made creams in the kitchen with my father." She enjoyed it, but she didn't find her direction until she took a summer course with the Carita sisters, renowned beauticians, while she was at the École des Beaux-Arts. The sisters were eminent talent spotters. Terry was sent to assist at a *Vogue* fashion shoot, kicking off her ten-year career as a makeup artist. She joined YSL in 1985, where she became the guru of maquillage to the rich and famous.

"Celebrity clients would send their private jets to bring me to New York to do their faces for a party," she remembers. As part of her collaboration with one such patron and friend, the late Marie-Hélène, Baronne de Rothschild,

"I would bring her the company samples that were too extravagant to produce in quantity, and she would choose some that I made uniquely for her—and she treated those little pots like diamonds!" When Terry founded her own firm, that experience sparked the idea for personalized makeup, which she now sells alongside her ready-to-wear line.

Her latest project is a collection of bed linens and tableware for the home, launched in 2002 and so far carried only in some of her French boutiques. It was born when friends admired what she'd designed for herself and urged her to go public.

Today the de Gunzburgs' dining table is laid with linen place mats, millefiori glass bowls, Murano-glass goblets and a *terre-noire* china service enameled exclusively for Terry with a lacy motif—all are items from her home collection. The setting is as beautiful when the boys bring schoolmates home for lunch as it is for dinner parties of twenty, when artists and photographers might be seated with bankers and scientists—and with a certain decorator, of course.

In its present incarnation, the de Gunzburg house is "an extremely sophisticated fantasy for cultivated people who love beautiful things," summarizes Grange. "Their vision corresponds exactly to what I like personally. It's a house I adore. I could live there tomorrow."

EAST SIDE DIARY

OVERLEAF: In the New York City town house of Spike and Tonya Lewis Lee, family photos fill a wall of the living room. The neoclassical marble fireplace is original to the house, which the Lees restored with architect Max Bond.

RIGHT: Most New York town houses have back gardens, but the Lees' place has a very lush internal courtyard.

T ONYA LEWIS LEE DIDN'T WANT TO LIVE IN Brooklyn. This was tantamount to heresy. Tonya, after all, is married to Spike Lee, the director of such films as *She's Gotta Have It*, *Malcolm X* and, most recently, *She Hate Me*. Spike is well known as a black activist, a provocateur—and a Brooklynite.

Tonya didn't have anything against Brooklyn, but it was hard to live there as Spike's wife, in Spike's very well-known brownstone, in a community that thought of Spike as its own property. She had nothing against being well known, either; but she drew the line when strangers started ringing her doorbell at four in the morning.

"Kids would stand in the street and yell up, 'Yo, Spike!'" Tonya recalls. "I would look out the window and they would say, 'Are you T-Boz?'"—a singer in the group TLC.

Tonya does have the aura of a star: a model's willowy build, an easygoing, natural warmth in her dealings with the world. But rather than being a performer, she's a lawyer, television producer, writer and hands-on mother of two children (son, Jackson, and daughter, Satchel). And although she leads a high-profile life, she wanted a slightly less public arena for it. "We needed to create our own family existence," she says. In Manhattan.

Easier said than done in the city's competitive real-estate market. When they started their search, in the mid-1990s, trendy

neighborhoods like SoHo and TriBeCa seemed overpriced. After a year and a half of looking downtown, she decided to broaden the field. "My mother and father kept telling me to consider the Upper East Side," she says. "I thought, 'Why would I want to live on the Upper East Side?'"

The answer begins on a sunny, tree-lined street, where the smooth stucco facade of an Italianate palazzo, quietly incongruous among brownstones and apartment buildings, shimmers behind an iron gate. Inside, a looking-glass world seems far larger than even the broad facade indicates: 9,500 square feet, with one big, comfortable room after another. Just across the threshold, an original hardwood floor, freed from the surfaces that covered it for years, gleams richly. In the living room, marble herms with the oval faces and full lips of Art Nouveau beauties support a fireplace mantel. And French windows open onto a private courtyard flooded with its own welling spring of sunlight.

Even for a die-hard Brooklynite, it was an easy sell. "I loved the house," says Tonya, "but Spike really loved it. He said, 'Oh, we're living here. What's our offer? Let's make it right here, right now.'" Tonya, whose father was a high-ranking executive at Philip Morris, adds, "I come from a very conservative family, so I said, 'You never do that. Are you crazy?' But thankfully he didn't listen to me."

The house's distinctive, spacious layout had attracted other artistic types before the Lees. Built between 1917 and 1919 for a Vanderbilt scion but rejected by her for being unfashionably far east, the house was empty when it was discovered in the 1940s by another Lee—the stripper and entertainer Gypsy Rose Lee. A later owner, the painter Jasper Johns, sold it to Tonya and Spike in 1998.

They may have been inspired by the energies of past residents, but the Lees took the house in hand, both restoring it—uncovering a wealth of original detail in the process—and giving it

their own stamp. Working with architect Max Bond, they moved walls, turned Johns's studio into their dining room, relocated the kitchen to a more central area on the ground floor and lived in the front wing of the house (now Spike's and Tonya's offices) while the back was being converted into bedrooms. Bond helped select a palette of cool, calming dove and blue-grays for the walls of the public rooms, where Louis XIV mingles with basketball memorabilia. The subdued but strong wall colors are also a perfect backdrop for the Lees' extensive collection of art by African Americans. Two bright Romare Bearden watercolors grace the master bedroom; Gordon Parks photographs line a hallway; and in the living room, the family photos that cover one wall face prints and lithographs by Charles Wilbert White, Charles Alston, Elizabeth Catlett—and Satchel Lee. "People say, 'Oh, that's such great folk art,'" says the artist's mother, amused.

Juxtaposing great art and family souvenirs, infusing an imposing and beautiful space with a sense of comfort and a cozy mess of children's toys: the combinations Tonya has created in decorating her home are reflected in the wide variety of roles she plays in her daily life. As a professional, she produces shows like the documentary *I Sit Where I Want*, an exploration of racial integration in a New York State high school that aired on cable television on the fiftieth anniversary of *Brown v. Board of Education*. As a volunteer, she sits on the boards of such organizations as the Legal Defense Fund of the NAACP. As a mother who chooses not to have live-in help, she maintains homes in New York and Martha's Vineyard, and she takes an active role in the education of her children, who attend one of the most competitive private schools in the city. Tonya's lifestyle, real-estate search and neighborhood have played into her most recent project, the novel *Gotham Diaries*, a contemporary satire of black upper-class society in New York, coauthored with Crystal McCrary Anthony. Tonya insists that the novel, published in 2004, is not a roman à clef, but, she concedes, "You write what you know."

Future projects include more novels and children's books, including one about a child with a dog—which excites Jackson, since his mother's commitment to writing about what she knows might necessitate the acquisition of a puppy. "I told my editor, 'You are really backing me into a corner here,'" Tonya says with a laugh.

But there are plenty of corners to back into in the house—including a few in which Jackson claims to have spotted the specter of Gypsy Rose Lee herself. "There's a good lineage to this house," Spike says. "I never ever thought I'd live on the Upper East Side. We didn't choose the neighborhood; we chose the house. Or it chose us."

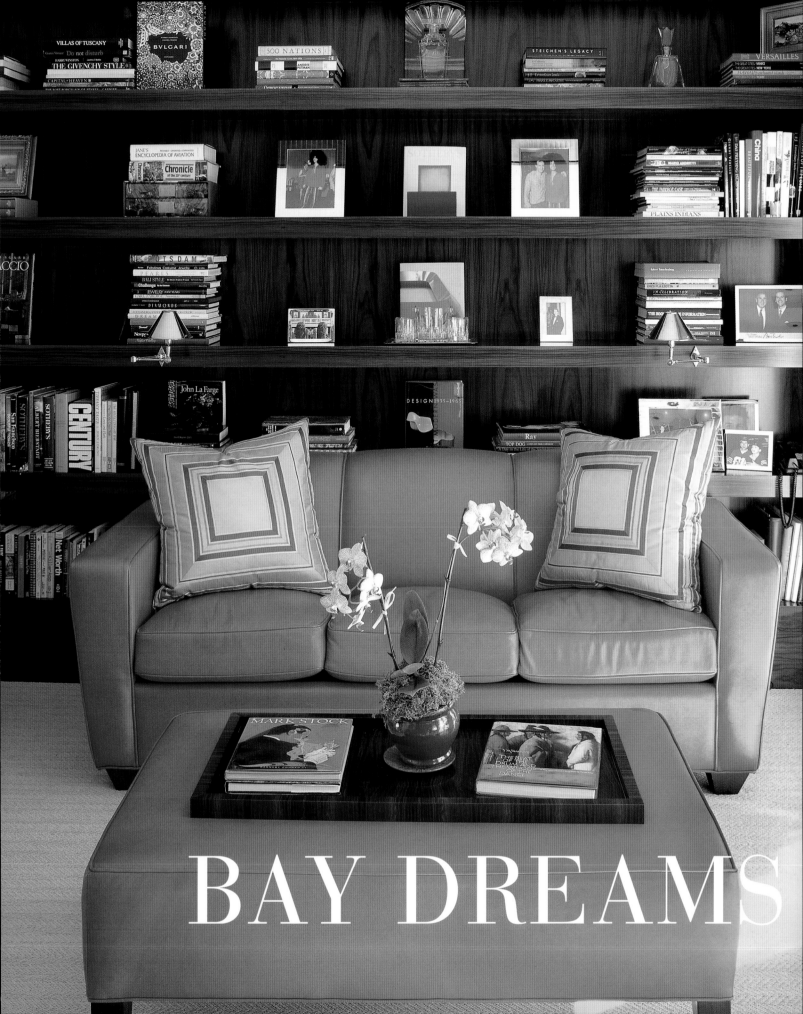

BAY DREAMS

OVERLEAF: An Old Master painting by Joseph Heintz surmounts Trevor Traina's living room mantel (left); Rosewood shelves line the library (right).

RIGHT: By day or night, a new sky-lighted atrium is the most dramatic space in the Traina house. It was formerly an open-air courtyard.

F OR EVERY PERIOD OF ONE'S LIFE, THERE IS THE perfect house. But as a bachelor in my early thirties looking to return to San Francisco after a stint in Seattle, I was hard-pressed to find mine. My hometown has great neighborhoods but surprisingly little variety in its housing styles; the choice usually boils down to the number of bedrooms, the placement of the kitchen or another such detail. I was looking for something more, something that would surprise. I didn't need the largest house, but I did want a place that was beyond the ordinary.

San Francisco real estate is distinguished by one thing, however: the views, with the area known as Pacific Heights ranking first in desirability because of its sweeping overlooks of the bay and the Golden Gate Bridge. Possibly the three most sought-after "view blocks" in the city are in Pacific Heights, the neighborhood where I grew up, on a stretch of Broadway known as the Gold Coast. It was here in 2000 that my real-estate agent and I finally found the property that I now call home. At first I thought it must be a bungalow—or was it a garage?—because no house was visible from the street. Once I entered, though, I realized it was indeed a four-story house, of modern design: a front garden led to a long hall with a dining room, living room and kitchen off it; the top floor had a

master bedroom, two master baths and a library; and the two lowest floors had guest rooms, offices and a family room that connected to a back garden. Tall and narrow, the place felt like a town house in Manhattan or Boston, albeit one that was hidden by the slope of the hill into which it was built. Best of all, every floor had views—some of the most spectacular I had ever seen.

The residence turned out to have been designed in 1962 by William Wurster, a highly regarded local architect of the mid-twentieth century. (Wurster Hall, housing the UC Berkeley architecture school, is named for him.) Though famously understated and simple, Wurster's houses are nonetheless full of character and style, noted for the architect's modern interpretations of classic floor plans and his sophisticated use of natural light. To be sure, the property, which had not been substantially redone by its three previous owners, needed work. The kitchen and baths were outdated. The master bedroom was small and faced the street rather than the bay. The dining room had gathered fabric on the ceiling. Some rooms were even painted Pepto-Bismol pink.

Still, it was obvious the house could be made into a home that would suit my needs. I loved the idea of such an understated exterior on a high-profile block. And the size was perfect: small enough for me to live there alone but large enough to allow for great entertaining and eventually to accommodate a family. And I was excited about the idea of exercising my current taste. I had grown up in formal houses done by notable decorators (including Valerian Rybar, Michael Taylor and Thomas Britt) that were full of antiques, bright colors and elaborate fabrics. In Seattle, I lived in an Arts-and-Crafts-style house that was furnished with antique Stickley furniture. I needed a break from clutter.

I wanted a modern home with neutral colors and luxurious but minimalist furnishings. I had purchased some furniture by Christian Liaigre for a previous house and was impressed by how masculine, handsome and timeless it was. I also was taken by stories I had heard about a 1930s Art Deco apartment on Russian Hill that Jean-Michel Frank had done for Templeton Crocker, the local banking and railroad magnate. I wanted what Crocker had gotten: the ultimate bachelor pad.

To realize these dreams, I needed help. Key to the process was Patti Skouras, a well-known L.A. and San Francisco decorator. Patti understood my lifestyle, liked the concepts I presented to her and took my ideas further than I could have alone. She and her capable colleague, her daughter-in-law Laura Blumenfeld, became my guides. We turned to Mark Thomas, a San Francisco–based architect, to carry out the renovation. Mark had impressed me with

his pragmatic approach and his knowledge of Wurster houses. Most important, he turned out to be a wonderful ally during the two construction-filled years that it took to achieve my vision.

To maximize the views, we added a new top story with a deck and a hot tub (we are in California, after all). We reconfigured the former top floor by moving the master bedroom to the back, again to capitalize on the vistas, and two rebuilt baths and a new library made the floor into a complete master suite. The living room below was given new paneling, copied from original Wurster designs in the front hall. The dining-room moldings were restored, and the walls were lacquered in a process that required sanding eleven layers (and using forty-five gallons) of paint—inhaling those fumes probably took ten years off our lives! The kitchen was totally gutted, and a new one was constructed by the Bulthaup company in Germany and shipped in sections. It was Patti's idea and is built like a Swiss watch, with drawers and cabinets that close precisely. It is unbelievably well designed and a total waste for a serial microwaver like me.

LEFT: Egg-shaped ottomans and Christian Liaigre window-back chairs offer prime spots in the living room for taking in a vista of the San Francisco Bay.

RIGHT: After finding a faded gem in Pacific Heights—a four-story 1962 house designed by William Wurster—Trevor Traina spent two years on its renovation.

When it became clear that, for the most part, my old furniture would not do for the new space, I decided to give free reign to my tastes and pick pieces from different eras. To complement my Liaigre chairs, sofas and desks, I bought early-to-midcentury pieces in New York: a 1920s Murano chandelier, '30s French chrome lamps, '40s Italian chrome obelisks, a '50s French lacquered chest and a mirrored console by Hollywood designer Billy Haines.

For consistency, however, we carried certain themes throughout the house: dark-wood furniture, window-back chairs or club chairs of varying designs, rock-crystal objects, obelisks. Those motifs and a stubborn adherence to a palette of black, white and shades of brown yielded a house with a great feeling of unity, despite art and furnishings from several centuries.

Even the guest rooms manage to continue the themes. Patti and I went back and forth on how to appoint them, but in the end we went mostly with her philosophy, which is that a guest needs good lighting, a comfortable chair and a desk for writing letters. I think she envisions David Niven in a dressing gown in a sturdy chair. While I hate to disappoint her, my friends are probably more excited by the large televisions in their rooms than by great artwork. A buddy recently checked into one room after a little too much wine and, for reasons still unclear to me,

awoke in another room. (There were no other people involved.) When he got up, I doubt he wanted to compose any letters.

My first evening in the house was far less eventful. After thinking the time would never come, I finally moved in one Friday afternoon in early 2002. Following a good night's sleep—in just one bedroom—I got up, took the elevator to the roof deck and grabbed a quick dip in the hot tub as the entire bay sparkled below me. Then I rode down to the kitchen in my robe—not my dressing gown—for a fast espresso from my unbelievably beautiful built-in stainless-steel Miele machine and called Patti to report. Although I was not writing a letter, as she would have liked to imagine me, or even perching in a window seat, reading the *New York Times*, it was still a great start to my new life in my ultimate bachelor pad.

STARTING ALL OVER

OVERLEAF: Two of Karen LeFrak's poodles lounge in front of competition photos on the fifth floor of her New York City town house.

RIGHT: Karen curls up with Mikimoto and Gem in front of Vicky Colombet's painting *Wind & Snow.*

FIRST THERE COMES THE CLATTERING RAT-A-TAT of perfectly clipped nails on the limestone floor of the foyer. This is followed by two hurtling puffs of white careening to an instant halt at the side of their mistress as she swings open the door. Being greeted at home by Karen LeFrak and two of her show poodles is a more animated event than one expects to encounter at a stately Upper East Side town house. But it is exactly that spirit of ebullience and discipline that characterizes Karen and Richard LeFrak's current life just off Fifth Avenue—a new chapter, as Karen is quick to offer, resulting from the couple's first change of Manhattan address in over thirty years of marriage.

The LeFraks' personal history has an old-fashioned, very New York ring: he was seventeen and headed for Amherst College and she was fifteen when they met at a winter dance. "Our parents were friends, and his father said Richard had to talk to me," says Karen. "All I remember is that he was tall, blond and smart"—and that he liked her sleeveless white mohair dress with pastel ribbons at the neck. They dated for seven years before getting married and soon moved into the same building as his parents. What else do you do when you marry into a family-owned real-estate dynasty? Then, as now, the LeFrak Organization was one of the largest private real-estate development and management companies in the country.

The formal dining room has its playful side, too, thanks to a wall of Picasso ceramic plates and jugs.

Flash forward over thirty-five years to the couple, now with two grown children, Harry and Jamie, who both work in the family business. Karen is active in a wide range of philanthropies; she has become well known for breeding standard poodles and taking home awards from the Westminster Kennel Club Dog Show. Richard now heads the real-estate company that was founded by his grandfather, Harry LeFrak, in 1901. He also pursues avid interests in contemporary art and architectural history while serving on several boards.

In spite of their many social obligations, the LeFraks have always been homebodies at heart. "Richard's is a very close-knit family, and I loved the feeling of safety," says Karen of those years spent living one flight below her in-laws, in an apartment on Fifth Avenue with a terrace overlooking Central Park. The Parish-Hadley decor was classic Manhattan taste of a certain stripe: a sophisticated country style that Karen refers to simply as "daisies and baskets with some English antiques." In fact, Karen liked it so much that she stalled for a year when her husband suggested they think about moving. But Richard truly wanted a change after his father's death, in 2003. "So I went around with all these real-estate people, pretending to look," Karen says.

The search was desultory at best, she now confesses, until she entered one particular town house. "The moment I saw the foyer, I knew," she

"I just knew I was home," Karen says of the moment she first entered the foyer of her new town house.

explains, sitting on the living-room sofa with one of the dogs, his muzzle tucked neatly under her thigh. "It was so serene and spacious and bright—I just knew I was home." The landmark neo-Georgian town house, built around 1875, had been completely renovated by Foley & Cox Interiors of New York for the previous owners, a young family that had barely moved in before putting it up for sale in the aftermath of a divorce. Best of all, it was a mere six blocks from their old home and offered a view of Central Park, if only a sliver, from one upstairs terrace.

They decided they wanted the house—and the talent behind the renovation, as well. Mary Foley and Michael Cox are both graduates of Polo Ralph Lauren, where they met while designing private residences and corporate interiors. "We have a philosophy of appropriateness," says Cox. "We believe in architectural integrity but also in updating classical vocabularies to suit living today."

"We're not design Nazis," adds Foley. "We don't have our way of doing things." In their renovation for the family that had preceded the LeFraks, they'd treated the town house with respect. They'd known how to tweak it in subtle ways, by supersizing the dentil moldings on the second floor, for instance, and switching out the carved-wood balusters of the first flight of stairs in favor of nickel-plated cast steel, touches that give the house a modern twist. The result was cosmopolitan and inviting. The LeFraks admired it so much—especially the subdued color scheme of white and cream—that they hired Foley and Cox to do more tweaking of a decorative sort.

The dining room got the biggest overhaul. For the previous owners, it had been a family room with a big television set and furniture for lounging. The LeFraks needed an event room for sit-down dinners. Or as Foley puts it: "Out went the Warhol; in came the Picasso."

Foley and Cox added a Venini chandelier and a custom-made dining table for twelve. They gave a bookcase cabinet doors to accommodate dinner services the LeFraks have collected over the years. And in the corner they installed a table for two that looks out onto the garden and provides a spot where the couple can eat when alone. "Add a lamp and some salt and pepper shakers and it's just like a romantic restaurant," Karen jokes. Upstairs, two bedrooms became a guest room and an office for Richard, while on the top floor, a playroom was transformed into Karen's sanctuary, where she keeps her dog-show trophies, a writing desk and her baby grand piano (she started playing at age three and now also composes). She calls it the Poodle Room.

From the start, the LeFraks saw their move less as a relocation than as a life-renewal project. "It was a spiritual reassessment, too," Karen says, "and the chance not only to edit our stuff but to edit our lives, our goals and our priorities." In other words, the decor had to reflect that with their children grown, the LeFraks were going to be spending more time pursuing their own interests. The second-floor library, with its gray flannel walls, softly upholstered sofas and sixty-inch plasma-screen TV, has become the after-dinner lair for Richard, a fan of sports and the History Channel. On the third floor, Karen has made an office for her philanthropy work and correspondence between the master bedroom and bath, which is itself a luxurious getaway, complete with a terry-covered chaise lounge. "It's my very favorite place for making phone calls," Karen says of the marble-clad room.

From top to bottom, the house is unified by its modern palette, a river of white on white on gray with dramatic dark-brown floors and quiet eddies of camel and beige here and there. The idea to go almost entirely neutral was Karen's, and it was a big break from the country colors of the LeFraks' previous address. The new setting complements the couple's collection of 20th-century art, which includes works by Artschwager, Botero and Avery, among many others.

The LeFraks' move has been as transformational as they'd hoped. Richard recently relocated his office from Queens to Manhattan and now enjoys walking to work, a stroll that also allows him to drop in on his mother each morning for a visit. Karen has gotten more serious about composing music and has begun writing children's books featuring an irrepressible character named Jake, a boisterous poodle with highbrow tastes. And she admits that one of the most unexpected thrills of a new life in a new home, even at this point in her marriage, has been the pleasure of new stationery engraved with an address that is finally theirs alone.

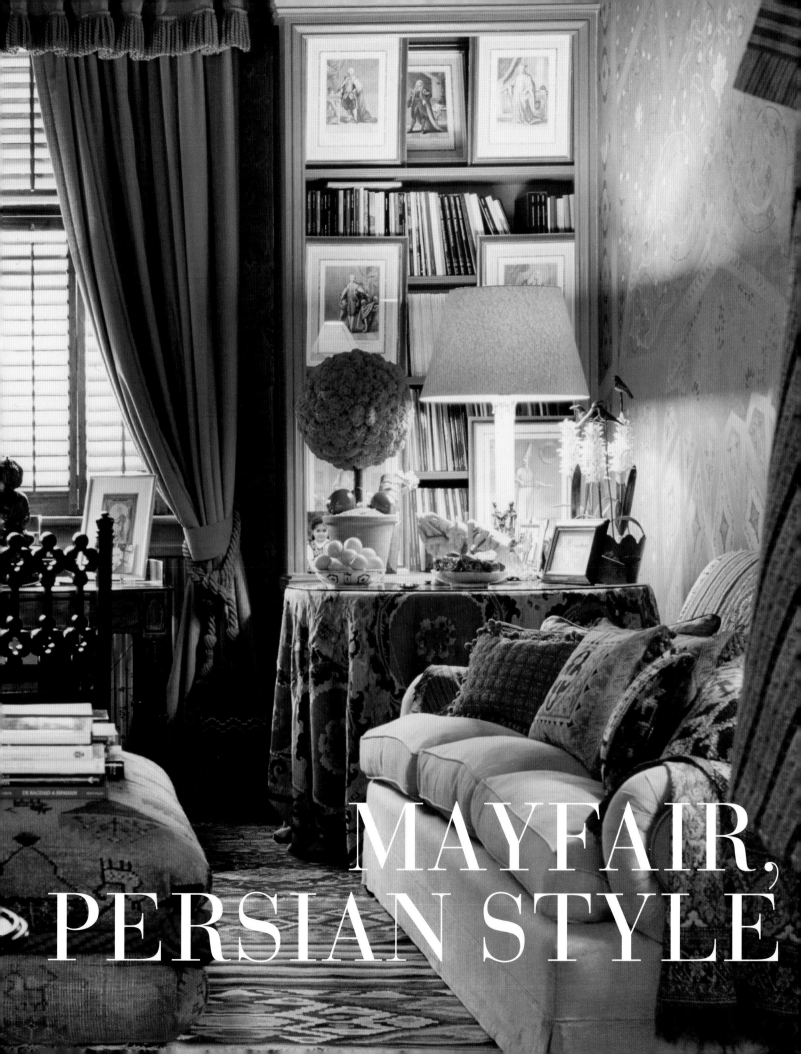

MAYFAIR, PERSIAN STYLE

OVERLEAF: Alidad's early career included a stint in the carpets and textiles department of Sotheby's, so it's only fitting that his London library houses an estimable collection of them—along with books.

RIGHT: The gold-printed velvet panel over the drawing-room sofa is from an 18th-century Mogul tent.

I N CONVERSATION WITH ALIDAD MAHLOUDJI, the adjective that most frequently recurs is "cozy." You might expect something more rarefied of a cosmopolitan aesthete born and raised in Persia, but nothing better describes the ornate fusion of East and West that has made him one of London's most admired interior designers and that is epitomized by the Mayfair apartment where he has lived for more than twenty years.

"In England," he explains, "you need womblike rooms where you can be warm and comfortable and relax; otherwise, you'd go mad with the gray skies and the rain."

The heart of his apartment consists of a red library and an ochery-yellow drawing room connected by double doors to form an L. Each brims with an extraordinary profusion of beautiful things, to create what Alidad (as he is usually known) calls a layered effect: neoclassical lamps and antique side tables; doors, walls and a ceiling painted with elaborate Islamic-inspired designs; above all, exquisite fabrics. From pristine new chenille to ancient, worn-out ikat, they cover sofas, chairs, floors and walls and even tumble from the tops of doors. It comes as no surprise to learn that Alidad started out in the carpets and textiles department of Sotheby's in London, or that it was his knowledge of fabrics that gave him the confidence to become a designer.

LEFT: Above the mantel in Alidad's dining room, a 17th-century portrait tops an antique mirror. The walls are custom-made embossed-leather panels.

RIGHT: The designer in his drawing room. The studded side table is from his furniture collection.

What makes this cornucopia all the more remarkable is that hardly anything matches. Alidad explains that his inspiration came from visiting stately homes: "I remember looking around these lovely rooms and thinking, that does not go with this. When you start dissecting it, you realize that there were once a pair of chairs, but one broke, so they brought another one that looked vaguely like it from another room. So this became my thing: I wanted my rooms to look as if they had evolved over the years, as different generations added different things."

Timeless Designs is thus the catchphrase appended to his company's name, Alidad. It is an approach to decor that seems, ironically, very much of the moment. But if he is hard to place in history, Alidad is also geographically elusive. "I always think of myself as a traveler," he says. "I was born in Tehran, lived there till I was about fourteen, then moved to Switzerland for a year, then came here. But in terms of where I am in a design sense—it's as if I've traveled slowly through Turkey toward Europe, stopping to pick up a bit here and a bit there, and I've come to London and learned about cozy living, but then perhaps I've gone back to somewhere like Venice, which was the melting pot of the two worlds [East and West]. I'm only happy in a place that accepts both."

In 1988, when he re-created his own red library for the British Interior Design Exhibition, the results thrilled the press and brought Alidad his first taste of fame. Nine years later, at the same exhibition, he invented an imaginary client for himself—tellingly, a stateless person living in a bachelor apartment surrounded by family heirlooms—and claimed his place in the top tier of London designers by carrying off every major award. Alidad now employs five full-time and three part-time staffers to help cope with the demand for his services.

"I would rank him at the very top," says Ruth Kennedy, the former managing director of Linley, David Linley's furniture company. She considers his prestige equivalent to David Mlinaric's, but adds that Alidad is a "really private"

On a library wall, the designer adapted an Islamic pattern combining stenciling and hand painting. The painting above the sofa shows Alidad in the same room.

person, which explains why he seldom appears in the society pages of magazines and never tells even his friends who his clients are. If he is now becoming better known, it is thanks to the recent launch of a small furniture collection and the introduction of his own fabric line, with Pierre Frey.

His success has allowed him to expand his original medium-sized apartment by acquiring the one next door and knocking through. One of the luxuries this has given him is a dining room where eight people can eat in splendor. Unusually, it relies purely on daylight and candles for illumination: a dining room, Alidad argues, can afford to be "dark and mysterious," since it is used chiefly in the evening. His is given grandeur by leather walls covered in a 16th-century floral pattern and a painted ceiling inspired by an Italian coffered ceiling of the same period.

Alidad remarks that he entertains less than he used to—"It's just too much effort"—though as Susan Crewe, the editor of British *House & Garden*, attests, he continues to lead an active social life. "There's almost no one in the industry who's as well liked," she says. "He's very well mannered and has terrifically high standards, but he's funny, too, and gregarious and hospitable. You can do yoga with him and then go off to a banquet together." While many of his friends, such as Nina Campbell, are from the design world, another visitor to his flat remarks that he is "someone who mixes really unusual people. You could find yourself sitting next to the porter from the Connaught or a princess from the palace."

The appeal of the apartment, adds the visitor, is that "you want to linger and touch and turn over and smell absolutely everything." This reflects another of Alidad's tenets: a room should delight all five senses. Not only does he choose fabrics that please the hand as well as the eye, but he makes a point of having music and a beguiling scent to greet visitors. "Then there is taste—I always have little nibbles around, because even if you don't eat them, you sort of taste them," Alidad says.

After two decades in the apartment, the designer has no desire to move. "For clients, I make decisions very quickly, but it's a pain doing something for myself. I can't decide on anything." He calls every one of his projects "one-off and fantastic, like haute couture," and prides himself on his sensitivity to people's needs. "If you give me the same house with a different client, the look will be completely different. No two people use a room in the same way."

However it turns out, the final product is guaranteed to have an Alidad stamp. "I'm doing a huge house in London, and the clients want one floor to be 1950s New York. I said, 'I'll do it—but it'll have to be my version of 1950s New York.'"

A cozy take on the Seagram Building? With Alidad, anything is conceivable.

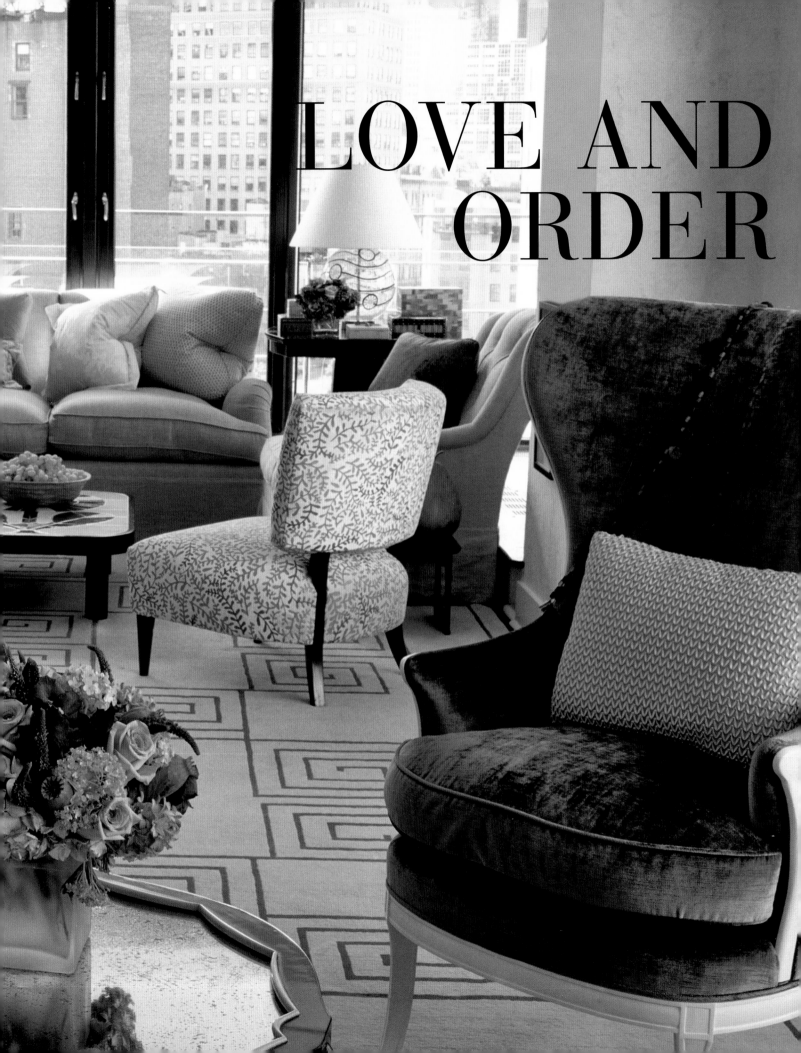

LOVE AND ORDER

OVERLEAF: Jeffrey Bilhuber's easygoing floor plan for Mariska Hargitay's New York apartment divides the long living room into three seating areas.

RIGHT: "Mariska wanted a sanctuary," says Bilhuber. A corner holds a portrait by Diane Arbus of her half sister with their mother, the late Jayne Mansfield.

I SAW THE PRECINCT ACROSS THE STREET, AND I thought, 'This is a sign—these are my people,'" says Mariska Hargitay, her face full of conviction as she describes her search for the perfect New York City apartment during the summer of 2002. Years of playing the role of detective Olivia Benson on NBC's *Law & Order: Special Victims Unit* had given the actress an unusual perspective on house-hunting, and so it was the police station—with the added bonuses of a rundown firehouse and a major traffic thoroughfare all within a few square blocks—that sold her on the condo. That it was in a new loft building, with exceptional light and views over lower Manhattan, was another plus.

"It's a great neighborhood—I'm always getting 'Hey, Olivia!' from the guys," says Hargitay, looking distinctively out of character as she lounges on a saffron-colored sofa in her apartment with her husband, fellow actor Peter Hermann. The two met on the *Law & Order* set and began seeing each other the weekend Hargitay moved into her new place.

"On our first date, I told her how thoughtful it was of her to put my initials up in her entry—there were the letters PH," says Hermann. "Of course, they stood for penthouse."

If their acting careers hadn't brought them together, the laws of natural selection might have. A more physically blessed

LEFT: The dining-room furniture includes an Edward Wormley sideboard and ebonized table and chairs.

RIGHT: "Did Jeffrey mention he got us pregnant by hanging an ostrich egg above our bed? Our decorator got us pregnant!" says Hargitay with a laugh.

Lynda Murray, while they tried to envision a new, shared look.

"Peter wanted to do things himself, but I was thinking, 'We need help combining our lives into one space,'" says Hargitay. They decided to start by creating a library, since books were everywhere. A visit to the professionally pulled-together home of a friend on Nantucket was fateful: "We immediately wanted a library that looked like the little sitting room she had, with these massive squishy sofas in it. Peter went from saying, 'I don't want a decorator,' to saying, 'Get that guy on the phone!'"

And that's how they met Jeffrey Bilhuber, one of the few design pros in New York who could possibly upstage them.

"They turned the spotlight away from themselves and onto me—that was unprecedented," says the mediagenic decorator, who didn't mind in the least. ("Are you kidding? I get stage fright only when there's no audience.") Bilhuber works in a polished American style that makes traditionalism look like the next great trend. After over two decades in the business, he's begun to develop into a bit of a brand, with two decorating primers to his name (*Jeffrey Bilhuber's Design Basics*; *Defining Luxury*) and deals in the works for a carpet collection with Stark and a bedding line with one of the big-box retailers. He agreed to take on a library for Hargitay and

couple would be hard to find. She inherited breathtaking curves and a Pepsodent smile from her parents, platinum-blond screen siren Jayne Mansfield and Mr. Universe of 1955, Mickey Hargitay. Hermann has the rangy, six-foot-five frame and pond-green eyes of a popular Yale crew jock, which, in fact, he was.

When Hargitay and Hermann married, in 2004, her two-bedroom apartment was big enough to accommodate an office for each of them and provide space for their healthy collections of books and photographs. They made do with Hargitay's existing furniture, selected during a collaboration with New York decorator

Mariska Hargitay, in her sunny living room, several months' pregnant with her first child.

see it. It comes from the painted ceiling. So I used the same trick in their bedroom." (Benjamin Moore 2013–70 . . . Bridal Pink.)

The eight months it took Bilhuber and his team to complete the apartment were some of the most charmed of his career. An astute listener and communicator, he was overwhelmed by the amount of content, both spoken and unspoken, that the two actors were capable of delivering.

"Mariska wears her heart on her sleeve," he says. "Her love for Peter and her love of her craft are contagious. The apartment needed to reflect that giving quality, which Peter has, too. To have been there during the initial 'love-in' was really moving. The passionate decisions we made together reflect that inspiration."

Some of the couple's favorite finds are a pair of tiled 1960s cocktail tables by Roger Capron, from Donzella, a sharp-eyed dealer in downtown Manhattan, and an amethyst bowl, from Ruzzetti & Gow, uptown on 72nd Street. ("I'm a believer that all great things come to New York, clients included," says Bilhuber.) Although very few of the pieces the couple chose are pedigreed, they have playful, midcentury-inspired silhouettes that give the rooms a young attitude. And Bilhuber managed to oblige on the color scheme: the living-room carpet is a pale, watery blue, offset by a pair of plummy velvet armchairs to either side of the fireplace.

Hermann, as long as they would consider his suggestions for the entire apartment. Case closed—jury decides in favor of Bilhuber.

There were a few stipulations, of course.

"I told Jeffrey, 'I'm from California; I need light and color,'" Hargitay recalls. "I love violet, and the ocean is my soul. I had no idea how it would all work, but he did. And I told him, 'We need to be able to take a running dive into any piece of furniture in this place and not have it hurt.'" Hargitay's childhood in Los Angeles must have been exceedingly formal.

Bilhuber recalls two more requests. "They said, 'If we don't get one of those gigantic sofas, you are toast.' And they wanted the pink glow I'd created in the Nantucket house. You can sense the warmth there; you can feel it, but you can't

Now that their first child is on the way, Hermann's office will become a nursery—without the typical frills. "I don't believe in decorating kids' rooms per se," says Bilhuber. "Just paint it a great, lively color and plunk the crib down in there. Whatever you do, there will be toys and clothes scattered around—and the baby will set the scene. All that 'My Special Pony' business is just icky." For the record, the couple will have a designer crib and changing table—from Netto Collection, a maker of Scandinavian-inspired kids' furniture, in New York.

And what about the cozy library/sitting room that brought this cast together in the first place? It was created in an alcove off the living room, complete with a sizeable plasma TV and a vast, cushion-strewn sofa. Hermann says it's his favorite spot in the apartment. "I think the books must talk among themselves when they're alone here at night," he says. "They've gotten to know one another by now, and it's unquestionably a great place to be." It's one he probably dreamed of being in during the six weeks he spent in London filming *Flight 93*, the story of one of the aircraft hijacked on 9/11.

With their home complete, Hargitay has turned her full extracurricular attention back to Joyful Heart, a foundation she set up in 2002 to help victims of sexual assault. Her TV alter ego is a sex-crimes investigator, and Hargitay receives letters every week from recovering victims thanking her for playing such an empathetic character—and for helping to broaden the public's understanding of this area of abuse.

"The mail I was getting made me see that there was a whole culture in the U.S. of young women feeling hurt and powerless," says Hargitay, who trained as a victims' advocate at Mount Sinai Hospital, in New York. From there, she saw a need for a program that would be a complement to talk therapy. Joyful Heart has partnered with rape-crisis centers around the country, and it is beginning to have the impact Hargitay had envisioned. It takes women who are recovering from sexual trauma through a series of activities that include art, movement and even swimming alongside dolphins, which Hargitay herself has found to be therapeutic.

Given the long days she and Hermann spend in front of the camera, portraying the sometimes tough lives of others, they feel lucky to have a home that restores their balance—something many people in their profession never get around to doing. "I feel that I've lived here forever and that we've actually done it ourselves," the actress says. "That's due to Jeffrey's gift for listening and for taking everything, and everyone, in."

In the decorating galaxy, it's also considered a star turn.

PLANNING A ROOM FOR LIVING

The problem with being in fashion at any one moment, whether it's with your wardrobe or your living room, is that, eventually, you're not. And though it can be captivating to ride on the roller coaster of domestic style, it's also a relief to step off and consider how you really want to live—for yourself, not for anyone else. That kind of thinking will eventually lead you to a home that is beyond fashion.

Ironically, the culture's current fixation on design and the decorative arts has made it challenging to formulate such clarity. We live at a time when design influences are everywhere, from TV commercials to online videos to bank offices, and it's easy to find yourself craving what everyone else is craving simply because it's in the ether. The best way to develop a more singular outlook is to repeatedly challenge your eye to see what it hasn't seen before. Why bother? For one thing, a living space that's personal and even a little offbeat is more welcoming—and sustaining—than one that might be confused with a chic law office. Second, a space you make yourself is a space you can change, and there are fewer creative acts more fun than rethinking your living room following an indulgent moment at the auction house or the local design shop. Eclecticism as a decorating approach is an implicit acknowledgement that the visual world is in flux; someone you might meet next week, or a place you visit, may yield up a new idea worthy of incorporation. It's a quirky and ultimately optimistic way of thinking, with a big payoff. Eclectic rooms don't date as much as ripen and mature over time.

ECLECTICISM:
HOW JACQUES GRANGE DOES IT

It's worth mentioning that even rooms "done" by decorators today tend to be looser and more eclectic than they were ten years ago. They can mirror a client's personality and have a whimsical edge; they can be accepting of the oddball lamp or the prototype table bought at auction.

Tour-de-force decorating in New York: designer Alberto Pinto mixes English, French and Italian furnishings from several centuries in a sitting room.

Jacques Grange created a new winter garden in a Paris house for cosmetics designer Terry de Gunzburg and her husband, Jean.

Jacques Grange is perhaps the most influential decorator in the world when it comes to mixing styles and periods. At it for well over thirty years, he has single-handedly revived international interest in French 1940s furniture, African stools, Belle Epoque pieces, and the works of Jean-Michel Frank and Claude and François-Xavier Lalanne, to name a few. His eye manages to find new delights for itself all the time. And sometimes, a client is the instigator.

For Terry and Jean de Gunzburg in Paris, Grange created a new winter garden with stained-glass doors inspired by Art Nouveau architect Hector Guimard, who had designed the de Gunzburg's house on the Right Bank. Grange furnished the space with fairly heavy, showstopping pieces that share an artful attitude: an Arts-and-Crafts bench, an ironwork planter, French rope chairs and a cast-iron table by Diego Giacometti topped with mid-century ceramics. This is about as far from today's popular "indoor/outdoor" look as it gets, no wicker or teak on the horizon, and yet the allusions to nature are obvious and real. The de Gunzburgs were thrilled.

ECLECTICISM, PINTO-STYLE

Paris-based Alberto Pinto is also famous for the omnivorous approach he takes to decorating. "I don't like what is very trendy right now, a decor that is completely monotone and empty—what people call 'Zen,' even if they don't know what that means," he says. "For me, to live like that is boring."

A virtuoso like Pinto has hypereducated eyes and a curatorial talent that allows him to combine furnishings he loves, usually of distinctly different styles and periods. After years of doing it for himself at home, he's convinced his worldly coterie of clients to follow his lead. Indeed, he has made it downright fashionable to be eclectic. That said, there can still be a profound difference between a living room filled with diverse objects and one filled with intimacy and emotional resonance.

WORDS FROM A WISE DECORATOR: ROSE TARLOW

"A house is what we design and decorate to suit an image of ourselves, and a home is what we establish by actually living there," says Rose Tarlow, nailing the importance of personality in the equation of good design. Almost two decades ago, the antiques dealer created a living room for herself in Bel Air, California, that has ivy clambering up its walls and collections lining every shelf—a virtual *kunstkammer* that could belong to no one else.

A LESSON IN PROPORTION

After furnishings have been taken into account in a modern living room, what makes it successful? To a large degree, it's proportion. Well-proportioned rooms are always pleasing. But when furniture and objects are being chosen for their aesthetic relationships, good room proportions are critical—without them, the "collection" you're curating will lack proper tension and drama.

New York decorator Bunny Williams, an expert in sizing comfortable rooms in new houses still on the drawing board, pays close attention to the scale of a living room when it's being planned and has developed some useful rules of proportion.

■ In traditional architecture, the larger the space is, the higher the ceiling can be. For instance, a small bedroom of ten by fifteen feet feels right with an eight-foot ceiling; if the room gets any bigger, the ceiling height should go to nine feet or more.

■ A big room, say one thirty by fifty feet, can take a dramatically high ceiling. But beware, says Williams, of going above fifteen feet without a cornice or other architectural reference point for the eye to settle on, or the room will start to feel like a well.

■ In modern and contemporary architecture, glass walls can mitigate the effects of a low-ceilinged living room, even

Rose Tarlow's Bel Air living room, accessorized with trailing ivy, makes a quirky and soulful statement.

A simple furniture plan can be elegant when properly scaled to the room, as designer Barbara Barry proves in this Palm Springs project.

when it's large. Still, a height of ten feet or more adds exponentially to the pleasure of being in a large room of any style.

■ If you don't have the luxury of new construction in your future—or of choosing a different room in the house to serve as your living area—Williams notes that there are techniques for "improving" proportions as far as the eye is concerned. In a low-ceilinged room, try hanging pictures or a large mirror up to the ceiling to make it look higher.

■ In a room whose ceiling soars, avoid scaling up all the furniture or you'll feel like a doll. A few big pieces will help; then vary the sizes of the remaining furniture, for excitement and balance.

■ The following solution illustrates the "more is more" logic behind Williams's preceding rule. In the great room of the Dominican Republic house she recently designed for herself, Williams commissioned an artist to paint four botanical scenes on canvas, one for each corner of the room. They measure seven feet tall; when hung to a height of ten feet, they act to anchor the gaze at that level, providing a natural reference point below the fifteen-foot-tall cornice.

FOUND: A GREAT FURNITURE PLAN

A second element of the successful modern living space is a furniture plan that allows the space to function in several different ways at the same time and still look pulled together. "Living" right now might translate into taking a phone call, working at a desk, watching TV, reading, napping, sharing a buffet lunch with a few friends, entertaining a crowd or playing on the floor with a toddler. Can one space do it all? Some professionals prove it can, and make it look easy. Jeffrey Bilhuber is one of them. Here are his key ideas for laying out a successful room of your own.

■ A furniture plan should "direct traffic" to various areas of the room, where individual pieces can suggest the activities they're suited for. Makes perfect sense—don't most people

already live this way? No, actually. A Le Corbusier daybed all by itself in the center of a room is a staple of Modernist decor. And yet without a lamp nearby, it wouldn't make much of a place to read; without a more private corner to harbor it, it would make a pretty conspicuous place for a nap.

■ When furniture becomes art for art's sake, a room ceases to be functional and can't support even one purpose, let alone many. Think about this in the context of your own space. Is it pretty—and unwelcoming? Such arch decorating is anathema to Bilhuber.

■ Try a creative, asymmetrical furniture plan, Bilhuber's signature. Such a plan is often set in motion by the deployment of two sofas, one larger, one smaller, in the living room. At least one of the sofas should be pushed up against a wall. When this arrangement is used in a rectangular room, the center is opened up for traffic and large-scale entertaining; one corner is left free for a multifunctional table or desk.

■ "Less is not more," Bilhuber likes to say. "Most people believe that the less furniture you put in a room, the larger it will look. In fact the opposite is true: rooms actually look bigger with furniture in them than when they're empty."

Three distinct seating areas downplay the grandeur of a New York living room conceived by Jeffrey Bilhuber—and they also make it multifunctional.

119

A Manhattan loft designed by Cristina Grajales features iconic pieces by disparate midcentury designers Jean Prouvé, Jean Royère and George Nakashima.

■ Here's an example of the designer's solution in action. In a Manhattan apartment for a film producer and her husband, Bilhuber downplayed the grandeur of the large, traditionally detailed living room by creating three discrete seating areas: a sofa, chairs and coffee table near the fireplace, the most traditional focus; another similar grouping near a bright window; and a square table surrounded by four chairs in a dark corner. Fifty years ago, the table might have been used for bridge; today it's Ming-period Chinese, and it can become a dining table or an impromptu desk for a laptop as needed.

AT LONG LAST: COMFORT

Which leads to the final ingredient in a successful modern room. If you can't relax at home, then it must be time to move. Quite a few of Los Angeles designer Michael Smith's clients like to do things like pad around in their pajamas during the day, nurse a baby or tune up their vintage guitars in the living room. No wonder his interiors always seem to feature multiple down-filled sofas, small tables beside chairs, adjustable table lamps and multifunctional pieces like ottomans, stools and nesting tables.

Few decorators devote as much energy as Smith does to providing his clients, many of whom are in the entertainment industry, with easygoing rooms.

"I don't believe in theatricality," he says. "It's just hard to live with. We, as a society, have so little leisure time. And my clients have even less than average. At some point, everybody takes off the stage makeup and turns on the TV."

Smith's understanding that comfort and ease result from spaces that are nurturing, rather than impressive to others, is a distinctly up-to-date one.

"That old idea of 'drop-dead chic' takes a lot of Formula 409 to maintain, you know what I mean?" he jokes. "Besides, who wants to make somebody else drop dead? That kind of competitive decorating is over."

In his own L.A. house, Michael Smith fearlessly combines a klismos-style chaise, a Flemish painting, an Indian bedspread—and a TV.

CHAPTER TWO
IN THE
COUNTRY

I N 1846, WHEN *TOWN & COUNTRY* FIRST STARTED PUBLISHING (it was known as *The Home Journal* until 1901), the concept of "country" didn't quite mean what it does today. There was city, there was country, and then there was wilderness— and the United States had an awful lot of the last one. Country meant rusticity and a comfortable setting in nature, a quiet place much better-suited than the city to "physical up-building" through woodland walks, golf, tennis and, for some, the luxury of catching healthful breezes on an outdoor sleeping porch.

Today "country" can refer to any spot a stone's throw beyond the suburbs, and "wilderness" often translates into a national park. But that doesn't stop us from holding onto the romantic ideal of living a simplified, somehow improved life in nature. And though the settings we choose aren't exactly cabins on Walden Pond, they represent the freedom Henry David Thoreau was so drawn to in the New England woods.

For some people, like Peter and Suzanne Pollak of Beaufort, South Carolina, that freedom has encouraged them to choose a historic antebellum house and a slow-lane life in tune with the past. For others, freedom can provide a chance to escape the pressures of conforming to a pervasive local style—as Nancy and Dan Brody discovered when they opted to build a glass house in the foothills of Virginia's Blue Ridge mountains, better known as Thomas Jefferson country. Perhaps the truest definition of country life today is the right to exercise our options. This chapter celebrates those who have decided to express themselves, in all their diversity and idiosyncrasy, through the houses they love.

At the Simon home in Montecito, Santa Ynez foothills rise behind the topiary garden, designed by Florence Yoch in the 1920s.

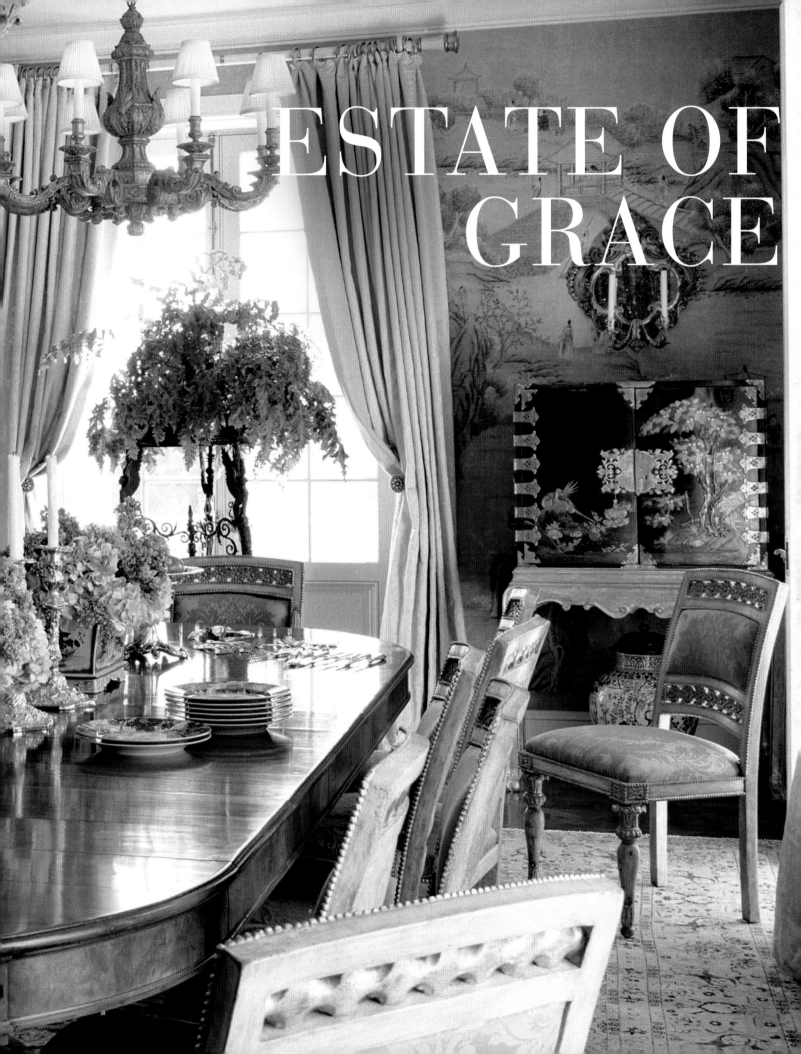

ESTATE OF GRACE

OVERLEAF: The Montecito, California, dining room of Bui and Herb Simon has a transporting effect, thanks to scenic Chinese-patterned wallpaper comissioned by interior designer Michael S. Smith.

RIGHT: Tuscan allusions are pervasive in the living room, where an Italian-school painting tops a console table displaying objects in the spirit of the grand tour.

B

UI SIMON STANDS IN HER MONTECITO topiary garden, her high heels buried in gravel. "I love these guys," she says of the boxwood birds and other whimsical animals that seem to be suspended in the scented air. "Aren't they amazing? When a few of them were ruined during our wedding party, our head gardener just put new ones in place, and chop, chop, chop! He's Edward Scissorhands."

Bui moved into Il Brolino ("the hedge") two years ago; her husband, Herbert Simon, has lived here since 1989. Along with head gardener Lalo Perez (in residence since 1979), they are the current stewards of a landscape designed by Florence Yoch almost eighty years ago and now considered a Montecito landmark. At its center is a shell-pink Italianate villa built in 1922 for Mary E. Stewart, daughter of a Chicago lumber baron. And that, in a nutshell, is Montecito: charmed estates built between 1890 and 1930 for a new leisure class that traveled west in search of warm winters and peace of mind. Montecito must have seemed like the ideal spot. It was about two hours north of Los Angeles on the freshly laid Southern Pacific Railroad tracks and adjacent to the coastal city of Santa Barbara, where the California Channel Islands beckon like dependencies off the Amalfi coast. Bounded by the Santa Ynez foothills on one side and the Pacific on the other, Montecito was just wide

enough for young American fortunes, like those of the Armour, Morton, Libbey and Fleischmann families, to transform its sloping acreage, the West Coast's version of Newport. Today the hedges and the fortunes behind them are larger still.

Bui and Herb Simon's house is one of about two dozen in the area credited to George Washington Smith, a local architect whose adaptations of Mediterranean colonial style have come to epitomize the Montecito look. Though its front facade wears the poker face of a 17th-century Tuscan stronghold, the parts of Il Brolino hidden from public view soften into a smile, with filigreed ironwork railings and a series of idiosyncratic terraces that speak the language of courtly romance. When the villa was finished, critic Rexford Newcomb, writing in the magazine *Western Architect*, noted that "Mr. Smith in a most interesting way has interpreted [an] Old World tendency without sacrificing anything that an orderly American housewife would demand under the head of efficient planning."

That would be Mrs. Herbert Simon to a T. Organizational skills come naturally to Bui, one of those rare people who can actually pull off the infinite challenges of a glass-front refrigerator. Bui keeps things humming here and at the Simons' house near Los Angeles, where they spend Tuesdays through Thursdays (Il Brolino is their weekend place). The beneficiary of this

systemization is Herb, who, as one of the principals of the Simon Property Group, a $27 billion retail and real-estate investment and management company, has a peripatetic schedule. Lately he's let go of many of the company's day-to-day operations as he directs strategic initiatives in Europe and spends time at home with the couple's eight-month-old son, Sean Robert (he also has children from two previous marriages).

Though Montecito is their weekend retreat, the Simons consider themselves most at home here. It's a cozy milieu in which everyone, no matter how low-key, seems less than two degrees of separation away from renown. As a philanthropist for Third World education and the 1988 Miss Universe (representing Thailand), Bui is a solid complement to her husband.

"People live in L.A. because they feel they need to be there—for opportunity, to enhance their careers," says the Thai-born American, who grew up in Pasadena and Bangkok and graduated from Pepperdine University. "When it comes to Montecito, first you have to build your success elsewhere, then you come here to enjoy it."

And to enjoy it properly, you need the right house. Herb already had it when he met Bui, though they agreed the interiors were languishing somewhere short of perfection. Enter the second Mr. Smith in Il Brolino's life, decorator Michael S. Smith of Los Angeles.

specializes. "The Simons have a romantic sensibility, and they wanted the house to be gracious and classical," he volunteers. "They also wanted a family house, but one that would be dramatic enough to leave an impression. Herb hosts Sunday breakfasts in the kitchen for his friends, for example—but they also held their black-tie wedding in the backyard.

"The thing about Montecito," continues the southern California native, "is that it looks like Lake Como or Fiesole or Positano, like your most idealized vision of Italy. It's very lush, with that enamel-blue sky. The best houses here were built inland, not on the ocean as they were in Newport, so they could be surrounded by gardens in the Mediterranean style. But the inside of Il Brolino was quite plain and more English than Italian, in the fashion of the time it was built. My job was to make the interior of the house correspond better with the exterior."

This largely meant dealing with surfaces, since the plan of the house already worked perfectly: public rooms on the ground floor, along with the kitchen, family room, media room, library and two home offices, and seven bedrooms upstairs. One of Smith's earliest moves was to commission decorative finishes that would serve as a background score for the antiques, art and objects to follow. And so the entry hall was was painted to resemble cut stone, and the

Smith launched his career in the mideighties by crafting modest-looking houses for immodestly successful people in Hollywood. More recently he's taken on projects for clients who thrive on richer domestic fare: a grand Manhattan duplex for Sir Evelyn and Lady de Rothschild, for instance; a 165-acre Santa Ynez vineyard with a Roman-style villa for fledgling winemakers; and a Malibu estate of some 40,000 square feet for a financial strategist and his vivacious wife. So prominent has Smith become that he now designs his own lines of furniture, fabrics and kitchen and bath hardware.

While Smith could very easily have swanned in and reinvented the look of the house, that's not his style. And so the results speak of the kind of happy collaboration in which he living-room ceiling was given trompe l'oeil coffering in pearly tints of *eau de nile*. The paneling in the library was darkened, and custom wallpaper in an 18th-century Chinese motif was ordered from the London-based firm of de Gournay for the dining room.

"Renzo Mongiardino used to come into a house and give it sense of many past lives—that was important here, too," Smith explains, invoking the late Italian design visionary. (Quickly, before any delusions of grandeur can be assigned, he pricks his own balloon: "Though there are elements of Mongiardino here, I'm not going to start gluing semiprecious stones to the walls. My houses have to be comfortable, to embrace the messiness of life.")

Achieving the correct degree of casual magnificence meant taking his clients off on four separate European buying trips, touching down in London, Venice, Florence and Paris. They put together a collection of bold, mostly Italian, furnishings, including a few of the star lots from British superdealer John Hobbs's 2002 Phillips sale and statement-making giltwood pieces from Florentine dealer Guido Bartolozzi. Weighing in on the side of comfortable living (if hardly messiness), notes Smith, were "more countrified Italian antiques, like the painted armoire in the living room, which keep the interiors from going in the direction of one big goopy pastry."

No danger of that. Smith chose to work in a palette more Canaletto than cannoli, strong in aqueous blues and greens, pale siennas, creamy bisques and carnelian reds.

"They're gorgeous colors," says the decorator, who has been known to peek into a client's wardrobe closet before scheming the colors for a house.

Now that Il Brolino has finally been brought up to her impeccable standards, Bui is using it more frequently in her fund-raising efforts. After winning the Miss Universe title at nineteen, Bui established two foundations, one of which has since paid for the building and operation of three schools and a pediatric AIDS wing in a hospital in northern Thailand. Both the UN and UNICEF sought her out as a spokeswoman, relationships she maintained until 2000. "Bui is like the people's princess in Thailand," Smith explains. "She's mobbed when she walks down the streets of Bangkok."

The Montecito project was obviously the start of a strong mutual affection between Michael Smith and the Simon family. Now that the decorator has several other ongoing projects in town, he's been renting a small weekend house of his own. "Herbie says I'm doing it to be closer to him," Smith recounts jokingly. But who wouldn't want to hold on to a little bit of Il Brolino and, for that matter, Elysium?

A WORKING CASTLE

L IKE MANY PEOPLE, I WILL NEVER forget my first visit to Chatsworth, the ancestral seat of the Dukes of Devonshire and one of the most palatial of all of England's stately homes. It took place some three decades ago, when I was 23 and had been invited to a weekend shooting party by my godfather, Andrew Cavendish, the 11th Duke, and his wife Deborah (Debo), whom I knew only by reputation as the sister of the famous British authors Nancy and Jessica Mitford. Despite the fact that my parents were regular visitors there and that two of my siblings had stayed as children, I had little idea of what to expect beyond the fact that it was supposed to be very grand.

I drove the three hours from London in my battered old car, an Austin A40, which, because of the noise it made as it chugged along, my family had nicknamed "The Kettle." Arriving in the park, which lies at the very edge of the Derbyshire Peak District, just before dusk, I rounded the corner known as Sandy's Turn, just outside the village of Edensor, and got the same feeling in the pit of my stomach that countless travelers before me must have experienced. I was overcome by a sense of wonder and awe at my first view of "the palace of the peak," bathed in late-afternoon sunlight, making the great classical West Front stand out dramatically from the dark

At the South Front, members of the household, garden, and restaurant staffs—a group eighty-five strong—join the duke and duchess (seated). "One's whole life is devoted to a building like this," says the duchess.

silhouetted backdrop of steep hills and woods. I pulled off the road for five minutes to take in the scene and gather my wits, then drove with some trepidation up to the lodge, where an imposing porter in a dark gray suit looked me up and down as if to say, "There must be some mistake." When he did establish my credentials and let me through, the Kettle and I felt very small.

As it happened, staying at Chatsworth turned out to be every bit as splendid as I had been led to believe, without being the remotest bit intimidating. After Henry Coleman, the friendly butler, had unloaded my luggage from the Kettle (which might have been a Rolls-Royce as far as he and his footmen were concerned, so respectfully did they treat it), he announced that "Her Grace is in the Blue Drawing Room." It seemed to take a long time to get there, which I was soon to learn was a common feature of Chatsworth life. But the trip was worth the journey, for the charming family sitting room—decorated somewhat confusingly not in blue but in white and gold—was full of laughing, chattering friends, and always a wonderfully warm welcome from Debo. I was also quick to discover that the Tapestry Gallery, a corridor outside the Blue Drawing Room, houses what is arguably the best drinks tray in England.

That night fourteen of us sat down in the private dining room at a splendid table beautifully laid with silver and flowers, and surrounded

OVERLEAF: Cavendish family portraits by Lucian Freud, John Singer Sargent and others fills the expansive walls of the "blue" drawing room.

RIGHT: The quiet life of a duchess: "I wake up and do my own breakfast in my room, usually between 5 and 6 A.M. Then I take the dogs out and feed my chickens. Except for that, no day is the same."

by full-length portraits of Mary Queen of Scots, Charles I, Philip II and Henry VIII. I had my first taste of Debo's disarming sense of humor. When I asked her why she kept a rather garish jar of German "flavoring spices" in front of her, she replied, "Because the food here is so disgusting." After dinner, I played the piano, and there was a game in which one had to walk all round the Blue Drawing Room without touching the floor, only the furniture. A great deal of drink was consumed and there was much laughter, which echoed down the corridors long after most people were in bed.

I am happy to say that this was the first of many visits to Chatsworth over the years, during which time I came to know not only the Devonshire family and their wide circle of friends—drawn far more from the artistic, literary and political arenas than from the aristocracy—but the other family living in the house as well: that stalwart band of men and women who work day and night behind the scenes to keep Chatsworth both a home for the Devonshires and a beloved destination for hundreds of thousands of tourists each year. While regular houseguests are all well acquainted with Henry (the butler), Stella Mellors (the housekeeper) and Helen Marchant (the duke's private secretary), there aren't many who would know John Bingham (the head plumber, who keeps their bathwater hot) or Doreen Motley (one of the switchboard operators) or Ian

144

Stella Mellors looks after "the private side of the house"—the Devonshires' living quarters. These include two drawing rooms, a dining room, the duchess's bedroom (seen here) and several guest rooms, which go by such colorful names as Mrs. Bater's and the Plough.

Fraser-Martin (the silver steward). These and many others are the unsung heroes of Chatsworth, who work on what Debo, sitting in her delightfully cluttered office, describes as "the nonstop rota of jobs to be done here, which is why there are forty-two people employed in the house to keep it going."

In her delightful book *The House*, published back in 1982, the duchess memorably described the difficulties of running and maintaining such a vast "dump," as she would put it, where every problem is magnified simply because of its size. "The roof is 1.3 acres; there are 175 rooms, 51 of which are very big indeed, 96 of more or less normal size; 21 kitchens and workshops, and 7 offices connected by 3,426 feet of passages; 17 staircases and 359 doors, all lit by 2,084 electric light bulbs. There are 24 baths, 52 wash basins, 29 sinks, 53 lavatories and 6 washups. The total cubic living space at Chatsworth is 1,704,233 cubic feet. The total cubic living space in a typical first-time buyer's modern two-bedroom house is 4,726 cubic feet, which means you could fit 365 such houses into Chatsworth."

In addition to the main house, there are 105 acres of garden comprising (among other things) waterworks, a maze, an arboretum and a spectacular rock garden, all requiring a staff of twenty-three. In turn, house and garden are set within a 1,000-acre park—which furthermore is

ABOVE: Waiting in the wings (and attics and cellars) are rooms full of furnishings from residences the family previously owned. The decor at Chatsworth is "not static," says the duchess. "Ideas on arrangement and decoration constantly change. As long as Chatsworth remains a family home, this is how it will be."

RIGHT: Guest privileges: Books are personally selected by the duke for every bedroom. "But each should have James's short stories, something by Wodehouse and the *Oxford Book of English Verse*."

surrounded by a wall nine miles long. The logistics of running such a place are quite daunting.

In many ways, it is a miracle that any Devonshires are in residence at all. As a result of death duties—the dreaded tax so feared by the English landed gentry—the family was beset by colossal financial problems in 1950, upon the death of the 10th Duke. At that time all the assets that the family had built up over 500 years—mostly land, investments and works of art—were taxed at a rate of 80 percent. Over the next few years, desperate attempts were made to raise the necessary

148

millions of pounds by selling everything from property in London and large areas of land to rare books and paintings (it took the family seventeen years to pay off the death duties). What finally solved the problem was the 11th Duke's inspired idea of giving Hardwick Hall, the family's other great house, to the nation. When Andrew Cavendish finally moved into Chatsworth with his wife and three children in the autumn of 1959, it was the beginning of what has turned out to be one of the greatest periods in the house's history.

Chatsworth, which had not been properly lived in since before the war, is now alive again. One of the Devonshires' grandsons, Eddie Tennant, lives in the old Hunting Tower, an Elizabethan folly overlooking the main house, and when his sister Stella, the much sought-after model, spent Christmas at Chatsworth a couple of years back, she turned the dining room into a catwalk and modeled some of Granny's old clothes. Today, Chatsworth is under stewardship as strong as it's ever been in its history, and never has it looked better—even to the Devonshires.

"Every time I see the West Front, I get a thrill," says the current duke, a sensitive and courteous gentleman, who in all his many years of residence has never taken living there for granted.

Most importantly, as of 1986, the future of Chatsworth was assured by the formation of a charitable trust that will own and oversee the property in perpetuity. The apartments, both private and public, positively glow these days, and the garden and grounds have been completely rejuvenated. Every window frame on the south and west fronts now blazes with brand-new gold leaf. Chatsworth today is a tribute to both of the devoted families who live there and together labor for its continued preservation.

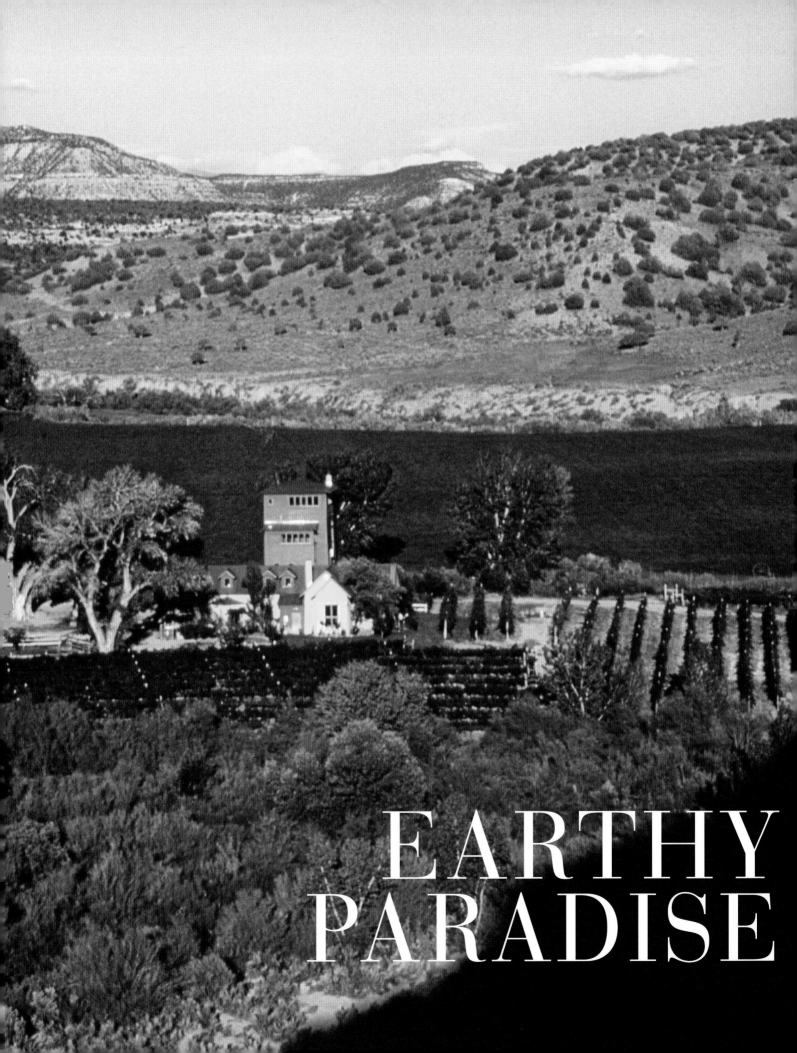

EARTHY
PARADISE

TRYING TO LOCATE MCELMO CANYON, COLO-
rado, on Google Earth is like giddily skimming the surface of the
moon over brown-cratered mountains and uninhabited desert.
Instead, on a U.S. road map, put your finger on southwest Colorado just where it nudges Utah, Arizona and New Mexico, and there
you'll find the magical valley where, in 1993, John and Emily Sutcliffe built their contemporary hacienda and winery.

This is Indian country, once home to the ancient Anasazi.
In fact, it was Native Americans who drew the Sutcliffes here in
1990, when Emily, an ob-gyn surgeon, came to work on the Navajo
Nation at Shiprock, New Mexico. There they lived in one of the res-
ervation's typical 750-square-foot cement-block houses while John
did some cattle ranching. Then he discovered a piece of land farther
east—eighty-eight acres in McElmo Canyon, near Cortez, Colorado.

They began to think of a house there, at the base of Battle
Rock, which, John says, was the "scene of the last struggle between
the Utes and the Navajo, who would jump off its cliffs rather than
face death by skinning, the Utes' preferred method." He adds,
"Some nights, local tribes still build fires high up in the caves on
Battle Rock, then dance behind them, casting weird shadows."

While Emily's commitment to medicine seems unwavering

(happily, the hospital in Cortez, near their land, needed an ob-gyn, so she moved), John's story has lots of chapters. Born in England, in Leicestershire, and raised near the Welsh border, he went to Sandhurst and became a proud officer of the Royal Welch Fusiliers. Hooked by tales of the American West, he then went to Oregon's Reed College. "I cowboyed in Nevada and Colorado before, during and after Reed," he recalls; then somehow (utter charm? innate sense of hospitality?) he became manager of Manhattan's Maxwell's Plum in its heyday—and then director of Tavern on the Green. Which led him to open restaurants of his own, in South Carolina and Georgia. Emily was raised in upcountry Beaufort, and she and John met in Charleston, where he would eventually own some ten restaurants, including a few designed by local architect Reggie Gibson.

It seemed not odd, then, to import Gibson to McElmo Canyon when it was time to design the house. "This area has such mystical touchstones: the cliff dwellings at Mesa Verde National Park, the spiritual Canyon de Chelly," says the architect. Gibson's design process entailed living with the Sutcliffes for weeks in tents pitched in a grove of graceful cottonwoods, where every little breeze set the heart-shaped leaves to dancing. "We needed to see what the house wanted to see, to hear what the house wanted to hear," he says. The result is a happy huddle—a single mass of connected rooms, each with its own distinct shape, all linked by a patio to a four-story Moorish building with the presence of a prayer tower. The house seems to grow organically from this dramatic, high-desert landscape.

Inside, the first impression is color, most excellent color, vivid and emotional; it's the way a sunset would look if it moved in and made itself at home. There's the serendipity of discovering through each four-paned window bits of the vast setting framed in small, deliberate pictures. "We had the luxury of spending a lot of time on the site," says Gibson. "We put the windows where the good things were!"

It is common to equate architectural pleasure with McMansion values—enormous scale, vast marble baths, windy entry halls—but rarely with this kind of nuance: the intentional placement of a window that lets sunlight spill onto a rosy wall, or how a front door painted just the right blue elicits a smile each time you open it. This house is what Southwestern style would be if it had never gone Hollywood.

To keep their house honest, Emily, John and Reggie Gibson took many rollicking road trips through the Southwest, inspecting the vernacular architecture they love and finding ideas to build into their home. They were so taken with the native use of the "shade house," a trellis covered with cottonwood branches cut and laid

OVERLEAF: John is thoroughly at home in the kitchen, whose cabinets are painted ten shades of green.

LEFT: The hacienda's high-ceilinged great room serves as living room, dining room and library.

RIGHT: Emily, an ob-gyn, practices at a clinic in Mexico; her trips south helped furnish the house.

across the timbers for shade in summer, then removed in winter for warmth, that they adapted this structure for the courtyard. ("Actually, I stole it," Gibson laughs.) They fell hard for tin roofs. When John and Emily responded to the added-on look of humble farmhouses, with each new room given its own shape, Gibson made models in clay, showing how the massing could work. For color inspiration, they turned to Battle Rock: "We collected stones and pulled those intense exterior colors from its very soil," he remembers fondly.

John Sutcliffe, cattle-herding cowboy and dazzling raconteur, is lying flat on his belly on the muddy bank of the irrigation ditch known as the Old Number One, struggling to replace the plug that allows water to flow into his vineyards. "It was all hard, dry cliffs here when we bought the land," he says. "The ditch is the reason we can have a winery here at all." And when he hauls himself up, soaked, he proclaims happily: "This is definitely not Bordeaux." The not-Bordeauxness of John's wine business is central to its identity, just as the intimacy of the house is worlds away from California's glitzy Wine Country chic. Because John's family in England has deep roots in the land, his transition to winemaker seemed like just more farming to him. Though he claims he got into grapes because Gibson thought vines running right up to the house would look great, the fine quality of the wine from his vineyard belies his protest.

Back home, as Emily talks about her work, her lovely eyes sparkle with the strength of her conviction; she radiates the humor necessary to carry her through a practice devoted to women unused to caring for themselves, mostly Native Americans, Hispanics and Mormons, some from nearby Utah. Besides working in Cortez, she commutes frequently to a clinic in Pátzcuaro, in the Mexican state of Michoacán. "We furnished a lot of this house from those treks, hauling Mexican floor tiles and finding pieces such as beds, cabinets, tables and old doors at trading posts and Methodist thrift shops," she says.

The Sutcliffes' kitchen is not so much designed as knowingly assembled, with ten kinds of weathered green woods for cabinets

and shelves, unmatched but very much at home, plus a red wall cupboard with doors like a pie safe's, which were made from the foraged spires of dried saguaro cactus. Emily's surgeon's hands sometimes pat out scones for tea on a black-and-white marble slab set on black cast-iron legs. "For all this desert life, this is a ridiculously English household," she laughs. Well-used pots hang from a high slash of red board. The kitchen's a deep, muddy Mexican red to its waist, a soft, glowing yellow above. "John painted it when I was away, and I came back and cried, 'You've made the bus station in Pátzcuaro!'"

The kitchen moves seamlessly into living areas—becoming the great room of a true hacienda, with its high walls hung with pictures to the ceiling—that in turn spill out onto the courtyard. Crossed dozens of times a day, the courtyard is the house's plaza, joining the living areas to John's office in the tower, but it is a sanctuary, too; its sun-shelter pergola, supported by vast trunks of peeled juniper, welcomes visitors and old dogs seeking the warmth of the tiles. On nights when Emily is not on call, the Sutcliffes will make dinner together, using watercress from the creek bed, chanterelles from the nearby forest, tiny potatoes pulled from Emily's garden; each of her beds is a welcome piece of geometry drawn on the land of this wild canyon.

John holds forth at dinner, referring to his Mexican foreman, Pancho, as "old chap," his Navajo workers as "lads" and his pals as "mates." He and Emily speak fondly of friends who never let the canyon's isolation keep them away. Friends like the architect Maya Lin and her husband, Daniel Wolf, who have a house in the area; the food writer Deborah Madison, who drives up from Santa Fe with her husband, painter Patrick McFarlin, whose work abounds here; Christoph Henkel, who owns the nearby resort Dunton Hot Springs (in which John, too, has an interest), and his wife, Katrin Bellinger, an expert in Renaissance drawings; and their friends the novelist Bella Pollen and her husband, publisher David Macmillan. Like heat-seeking missiles, old and new friends flock to remote McElmo Canyon—people who came for the wine and stayed for the charm. It's easy to see why.

161

LIFE IS BUT A DREAM

Long before I ever met him, Ralph Lauren was a part of my life. For years, I had slept on his sheets, dried myself with his towels, wore his clothes, applied his mascara and gave Polo shirts, ties and fragrances as gifts (always gratefully received) to the male members of my family. And although I have yet to paint a room in one of Ralph's new hues or cuddle up with a lion cub, as model Bridget Hall once did in his Safari ads, I hope one day I will.

After over forty successful years in business, Ralph Lauren is no mere fleeting phenomenon; he has become an institution, the very embodiment of the old-fashioned American Dream. Increasingly and strategically, he has expanded his empire abroad with the acquisition of a 45,000-square-foot building front and center on Bond Street in London as his European headquarters. Not bad for a boy from Mosholu Parkway in the Bronx—and he would be the first one to admit it.

He grew up Ralph Lifshitz, the youngest of four children, in a respectable middle-class Jewish family. Like many kids, he escaped to the movies on Saturday afternoons. The difference is that he wasn't content to go back to real life, as pleasant as it might have been.

On weekends, Ralph and Ricky take much-needed time together. Here, they are joined by sons David (far left) and Andrew, and daughter Dylan.

No one, probably not even Lauren himself, can explain exactly what set his sights soaring—what made him possibly think his dreams would be realized. It is more than a competitive spirit, which he clearly has. Or a self-propelled drive, which is still unstoppable. Or enormous talent. Or vision. It is, in fact, all of those things, and far more than the sum of their parts.

Those who work for Lauren—and I met many in the course of researching this profile—have a hard time articulating the essence of the man. He is beyond easy definition. But the one thing everyone agrees on is that Ralph Lauren never thinks in terms of individual products—a pair of jeans, an Oxford shirt, a throw pillow, an ottoman. To him, they are all part of the bigger whole: his world, his universe and—coming soon—his galaxy. Where it all starts and then leads is anybody's guess. Lauren's well of ideas runs deep, with no drought in sight.

At an age when he could be easing off and letting go, Ralph Lauren is instead revving up his engines. The biggest move was to buy back—and thereby have full control of—his women's-wear business, which had been operated for twenty-two years by Bidermann Industries under a licensing agreement. Licensing is common in the design world, but this particular agreement, Lauren came to feel, granted Bidermann too much power—primarily, the right to manufacture and distribute the women's-apparel line. Although he continued to design the clothing, he was not in control of the important decision making.

On the heels of the buyback, he also launched a new moderately priced women's collection, called Lauren by Ralph Lauren, in conjunction with the Jones Apparel Group; went into business with Rockport to develop high-tech footwear; expanded his Polo Sport line, focusing on Polo Sport for women; opened up a new Polo store in San Francisco; reenergized his jeans line; introduced a high-end division of imported cotton bed linens called White Label (equivalent to Purple Label, the line of finely tailored men's wear that he launched in the mid-'90s); and positioned the company for major growth in Europe with the building on Bond Street.

Who is this man, anyway? How did he go from being a designer of men's ties in 1967 to becoming America's stylemaker supreme? How far does his influence extend? Let me answer the last question first: his influence knows no bounds or borders. Ralph Lauren is almost as recognized in Europe and Japan as he is in the American West. And if he isn't yet, he will be.

An incredibly elegant woman I know—Swiss, by birth—is married to Englishman Martin Skan and lives in Great Britain. Brigitte—Brigi, as she is known—looks as if she belongs on the pages of *Country Life.* She is the quintessential

chatelaine, often dressed in a hacking jacket, riding pants and high boots. Ask her who her favorite designer is and she will say, almost surprised that you asked, "Why, Ralph Lauren, of course." (Like many Europeans, she pronounces it Lau-REN, putting the accent squarely on the second syllable.) Not Hardy Amies? Not Holland & Holland? No, Ralph Lauren. "He suits me," she says matter-of-factly.

A bright teenaged African-American girl from a suburb of Dallas has become a pen pal of mine. She had a summer job at the Limited, but that didn't stop her from spending "several days" at the Polo shop. In a recent letter she wrote, "I don't know if you knew this, but my favorite designer is Ralph Lauren. I've been wearing Polo since I was six. I have the loafers and all. Without overexaggerating, I have at least one of everything of Ralph Lauren's: jacket, sweater, blazer,

T-shirt, button-down shirt, sweat jacket, hat, cap, slacks, shorts, blue jeans, socks, tennis shoes, purse, wallet, umbrella, tote bag, key chain, teddy bear, undergarments, lipstick, backpack, towel, bedsheets, pillow, blanket, tie, mug, swimsuit, Frisbee, bathroom set, etc." Etc.? What's left?

There are, of course, detractors, those who accuse Ralph Lauren of being derivative—right down to the black-and-white photographs of instant ancestors in their silver frames and the Sargent-like oil paintings exhibited in his stores. To them, he is too neat, too new and—here is the coup de grâce—too nouveau.

Does this criticism bother him in the least? You bet. "I've heard this comment and I've never understood it," he says. "What does 'derivative' mean? I've seen fashion go from revivals of the '60s and '70s, to the '50s and back to the '60s. Gucci does clothes that I did twenty years ago. Is that being derivative?

"I do think there is a traditionalism to my sensibility. There is definitely a world I live in that I enjoy and respect. I'll pick from here and choose from there. But—in the case of England—I feel I was able to go back and give it something more." And then he adds, for emphasis, "Prince Charles buys my clothes, or at least he sends his butler to buy my clothes."

"There is a word for what I do, but I really don't think it is 'derivative.' I take something and I make it mine. I re-create it to my liking and to my taste."

I met Ralph Lauren in the flesh in the fall of 1995. We had lunch at Harry Cipriani, on Fifth Avenue and 59th Street, a block away from his offices. Until then, the only time I had seen him was on the runway, at the tail end of a fashion show, usually dressed in his designer-at-work uniform: a gray T-shirt and well-worn jeans. On this day, he wore an impeccably cut navy blue suit—from his just-launched custom-tailored Purple Label collection. With his silver hair and year-round tan, Lauren stood out in a very chic crowd, and, although he probably knew it, he didn't let on. While curious heads turned our way, he kept attention focused on me, asking one question after another, most of them revolving around today's upscale-magazine reader—his customer. I noticed that he ate lightly (a salad to start, plain grilled fish, melon for dessert, no wine) and talked deliberately—intensely at times, yet quietly and thoughtfully. Time and again, he made the point that he doesn't design in isolation. "Everything I do is a reflection of my life."

That comment is more than casual lunchtime conversation; it is his anthem—not only of Ralph Lauren, the man, but of Ralph Lauren, the company. And everyone who works for Lauren knows it by heart.

Buffy Birritella, senior vice president of women's design and advertising, who has been his right-hand associate for over twenty-five years, understood from the very start what he was trying to create and sums it up in a single word: image. "For Ralph, it is about creating a mood—not about a lapel or a shape. I identified with what he was trying to say with his clothes. I could see the literary implications . . . that a certain early look came straight off Gatsby's lawn."

To his brother Jerry, who is senior vice-president of men's design, what Ralph Lauren has become as a business is an outgrowth of what they were like as kids. "There was no grand design; we were just trying to find ourselves. We'd dream together early on. It didn't matter if we never went hunting or fishing; we could still spot a great leather jacket and recognize its gutsiness, or see the difference between a poor reproduction and the real thing. Growing up in the middle-class Mosholu Parkway, we played stickball, basketball and baseball and went to the movies— a lot. Ralph had a kind of ache . . . I honestly don't know where it came from. Other people went back to their lives, back to school, to their jobs. My brother kept dreaming. He never said, 'I want to get rich . . . I want to be successful.' He said, 'I want to make it better.'"

By that, he doesn't mean merely improving on a pair of spectator shoes or a cable-knit sweater; it is a *Weltanschauung*.

"Generally, I'm a long-term person. I'm long-term about my work. I'm long-term about my family. I'm a builder. Everything I do is an extension of my life. When I was looking for things to put into a new house, Ricky and I went shopping for linens. What I saw wasn't good, so I began designing sheets and towels for my family and me." That is how it usually begins, with his own dissatisfaction with what he sees in the vast marketplace.

His involvement in philanthropy also started in a personal way. Of his work with the Nina Hyde Center for Breast Cancer Research in Washington, he states simply, "It was because of Nina. [Nina Hyde, fashion editor of the *Washington Post*, died of the illness in 1990.] I'd had a benign brain tumor. She had cancer. I ran into her one day and she convinced me that, as a designer of women's apparel, I should be doing something to combat this illness that takes so many women's lives . . . that I had an obligation. It was her cry that reached me." He and Katharine Graham established the initial grants, and he has played an active role ever since—so much so that in 1995 he became the first recipient of the center's humanitarian award.

He speaks of his own brush with mortality: "It was in 1986. I was about to be on the cover of *Time* magazine and I was on vacation. I had a ringing in my ears [which turned out to have nothing to do with the tumor] and knew I had to face up to whatever it was. My doctor urged me to come home and go in for a CAT scan.

"Envision this: It's a beautiful day and I'm sitting in a hospital, isolated . . . out of the world . . . out of the loop. That's hard to deal with if you're as excited by life as I am. I still can't come to terms with somebody being well one day and then suddenly developing breast cancer.

"I've always been sensitive about life and am grateful for what I've had, but when I came out of the hospital I was more scared than when I went in—maybe because it dawned on me that anything could happen to me . . . just like that.

"I went back to work with a much greater fury. I had all this pent-up energy. Everyone noticed. I don't take anything for granted. Yes, I'm very involved in my work, but it has never blinded me from the people I work with or from my family."

On the home front, his personal life is solid—marriage to Ricky for over forty years has resulted in three beautiful, bright and, yes, incredibly likable and charming children (Andrew, David and Dylan).

Over the course of a year, there were many discussions about where we would photograph this story to give a glimpse of Ralph Lauren's private life—and, make no mistake, it is private. He rarely steps out, avoiding the very spotlight other

The dining room in Bedford is layered with paintings, photos and memorabilia.

designers bask in, and prefers to spend weekdays in the office and weekends with his wife at one of their country homes—either just the two of them or with one or more of the children. They have a town house in Manhattan ("very modern"), a lodge in Telluride, resort homes in Jamaica and Montauk, and a house in Bedford, New York. We settled on Bedford, with its more than 250 acres of property (ninety acres of which are mowed lawn), tall trees and a stone house that looks as if it were built for Nancy Lancaster.

The house was originally owned by a family named Fowler during the World War I years. But practically everything has been moved, redesigned and improved—Laurenized, as it were—to become "the house that Ralph rebuilt." It is, as you might expect, a gorgeous place.

Inside, the house is decorated in traditional Lauren—massive limestone mantelpieces; stone and dark wood floors; mahogany paneling; rich fabrics on the walls (lots of tartan plaids); animal paintings. It is a country squire's version of the Rhinelander mansion on Madison Avenue, which is now the Polo flagship store and showplace. The couple share a closet, lined in pool-table-green felt, in which everything is neatly organized and color-coordinated.

Our crew, led by photographer Victor Skrebneski, had been in Bedford for two days shooting the property and interiors.

By the time we broke for lunch on the final day, we had photographed several situations with the family, with more to follow in the afternoon. We ate outdoors at a long wooden table covered with a white linen tablecloth, set with Lauren plates and flatware. The weather was perfect, with a slight breeze. I look to my left and to my right and think, "This is a Lauren ad come to life."

Ralph was telling Skrebneski that one day he would like to make a movie. A movie? Why, of course. It is the natural next thing. He said he'd been looking at scripts but hadn't found the right one yet. But he probably will, so watch for it at your neighborhood theater. If Ralph Lauren has it his way—and I'm betting he will—it will be even better than *Gone With the Wind*.

INSIDE OUT

T HE BLUE RIDGE FOOTHILLS OF ALBEMARLE
County, Virginia, have a gentle, undisturbed beauty. As you turn
onto the private road that traverses Dan and Nancy "Nan" Brody's
260-acre farm, you follow a series of switchbacks around a clap-
board caretaker's house, pastureland bounded by white-painted
fences, a hazelnut orchard. Halfway down a closely mown valley,
you catch sight of your destination: a taut, serenely confident house
of glass, steel and Tennessee sandstone tucked halfway up the
opposite slope, with dense woods at its back. The work of New York
architect Bartholomew Voorsanger, the house, completed in 2004,
is the Brodys' discreetly contemporary lookout onto the past.

"We told Bart we had a great site and that we wanted the
house to be inside out," says Nan, a quietly forceful attorney whose
faultless manners, though instilled on the shores of Lake Michigan,
often cause people to think she's from the South. "We wanted to
experience nature from our living room. And we told Bart we didn't
want to have too much decor; the house would be the decoration."

What architect wouldn't fall for that?

"Nan and Dan came up to interview me in New York, and I
thought, 'I know they've seen my work, but they're from Charlottesville,'" Voorsanger recalls of their first meeting, in 1997. The

Brodys had come across one of his houses in a magazine and had followed up with his office.

"I started out by saying, 'I want you to know I won't be doing any Jeffersonian architecture.'" Voorsanger, a San Francisco–raised suit-and-tie man whose resemblance to FDR must disarm a few clients, studied architecture at Harvard and spent ten years in the office of I.M. Pei.

On his own since 1986, he's designed houses of muscular grace for some of the country's richest citizens. Diplomacy rarely eludes him. "You know, I happen to be a huge admirer of Jefferson," he says. "But I firmly believe that if he were alive today, he'd be Frank Gehry. I explained how I felt about this to Nan and Dan, and they said they understood. But I knew that the cultural

177

OVERLEAF: Tennessee sandstone anchors the steel-and-glass house to its hillside site and also defines a walled garden off the master bedroom, at right.

ABOVE: Nan and Dan (in University of Virgina colors) pause on the Brazilian-cherry stairs.

RIGHT: In the spinelike central hall, a wall of southern sandstone is skylit.

climate in Charlottesville would offer tremendous resistance to contemporary building. I was a little apprehensive."

The couple laid out a simple set of needs for themselves and their two teenaged sons, including living, dining and family rooms, bedrooms and home offices, the sum of which Voorsanger estimated at roughly 7,000 square feet.

But he wondered about their priorities. "We said that we wanted a two-car garage and three bedrooms: a master for us and rooms for Buck and Doug," recalls Dan Brody, a sandy-haired healthcare executive. "He told us we should really be thinking of a bigger garage and four bedrooms, for resale value. And I said, 'With all due respect, Mr. Voorsanger, if we're hiring you to design

In the master bath, the colors echo the view from the second floor window of the Brodys' farm.

our house, we're not in this for resale.'" With that, Voorsanger says, he decided the couple was "grounded in reality." They agreed to move forward together.

Though the Brodys had always lived in traditional houses, their decision to build in a style of their own time, rather than one that might suit someone else's Virginia ancestors, was not capricious. They'd considered building a modern house when they first married and settled in Dan's hometown, near Pittsburgh, in 1979. But a Georgian Revival that fit their needs came along, and nine years later they moved to Charlottesville. It was a familiar setting: Dan is a University of Virginia alum, like his father (a retailer who cofounded the campus Jewish center) and his grandfather. Because Dan wanted to live downtown and Nan preferred the country, they compromised on a comfortable Cape Cod in a subdivision, thinking they'd have it for a year. The location was so convenient and their lives with the boys so full, however, that it took them more than a decade to find and agree on their farm, which positions them among local royalty (John

Grisham, Dave Matthews and Sissy Spacek). The idea of farmland appealed to Nan and the boys; Dan was tired of waiting to build.

In a dozen meetings with the Brodys over the course of a year, Voorsanger developed a plan for the house (7,000 square feet, two-car garage, three bedrooms) that involved a pair of narrow rectangular volumes lying parallel, one slightly longer and sitting above the other on the sloping site, to provide west-facing views of the Blue Ridge hills from almost every room. The single-story uphill volume would meet the two-story downhill volume in a soaring hallway running sixty-two feet, the full length of the house. There was an aeronautical lightness to the scheme, in which floor-to-ceiling windows seemed to support roofs of tremendous delicacy, their corners upturned in a winglike flare.

Such dramatic form making is typical of Voorsanger. His houses are feats of engineering—and rites of passage for builders—that are often sited on open land or on hilltops. The Brody house is simple, comparatively speaking, the curving rooflines its only big gesture.

Underground, the architect had another innovation planned. "We've been using geothermal heating wells and cooling systems since the late 1990s," he says. "They're incredibly efficient and can offset a huge energy expense." He installed ten geothermal pumps on the Brody property. Though expensive to put in, the systems quickly make up for that by significantly lowering the cost of electricity. The architect also made several other moves toward energy efficiency on the house: All the glass is "low-e," meaning it transmits less heat to the interior. The window shades are timed to respond automatically to the arc of the sun, again lessening internal heat build-up. And the major building materials—lumber and stone—were purchased within 500 miles of the site, minimizing trucking costs.

Construction began in 1999 and stretched to five years, as the house proved challenging to the Brodys' contractor; then the English window supplier went bankrupt, causing more delay.

Voorsanger put the slowdowns into perspective for his clients. "The construction process is like driving. You can go as fast as you want, but the faster you go, the more dangerous it gets," he says. "The whole process of high-end building involves spending the kind of money that can have a serious impact on your lifestyle. For some people, it can put them in debt; it can break up a marriage. You're going to be making major, expensive decisions, ten to twenty a month, for a long time. They really add up, and you need to feel comfortable with them. A delay can actually help."

In 2002, as their second son, Doug, followed his older brother to U.Va., the Brodys finalized their furniture decisions and drew up a plan for trees and shrubs with Nelson Byrd Woltz Landscape Architects in Charlottesville. In both cases the goal was suitability: to the architecture, to a family with grown children and many friends, to the surrounding countryside.

As Voorsanger saw the project taking shape, he no longer worried about what the locals would think. "But I did question myself: 'Is it too relaxed?' Normally we deal with much more assertive architecture, on more dramatic sites. But in its quiet way, this house has extraordinary spatial substance and conviction about how all its pieces go together. And it is designed in response to a very subtle, very lyrical landscape. You don't walk in and say wow, but hopefully, by the end of a visit, you'll get to the wow."

The Brodys certainly have. One morning about a year after they moved in, Dan picked up the phone and called Bart Voorsanger in New York to tell him how happy he was to be waking up in the house every day. That there was at least one car permanently parked in the driveway didn't bother him at all.

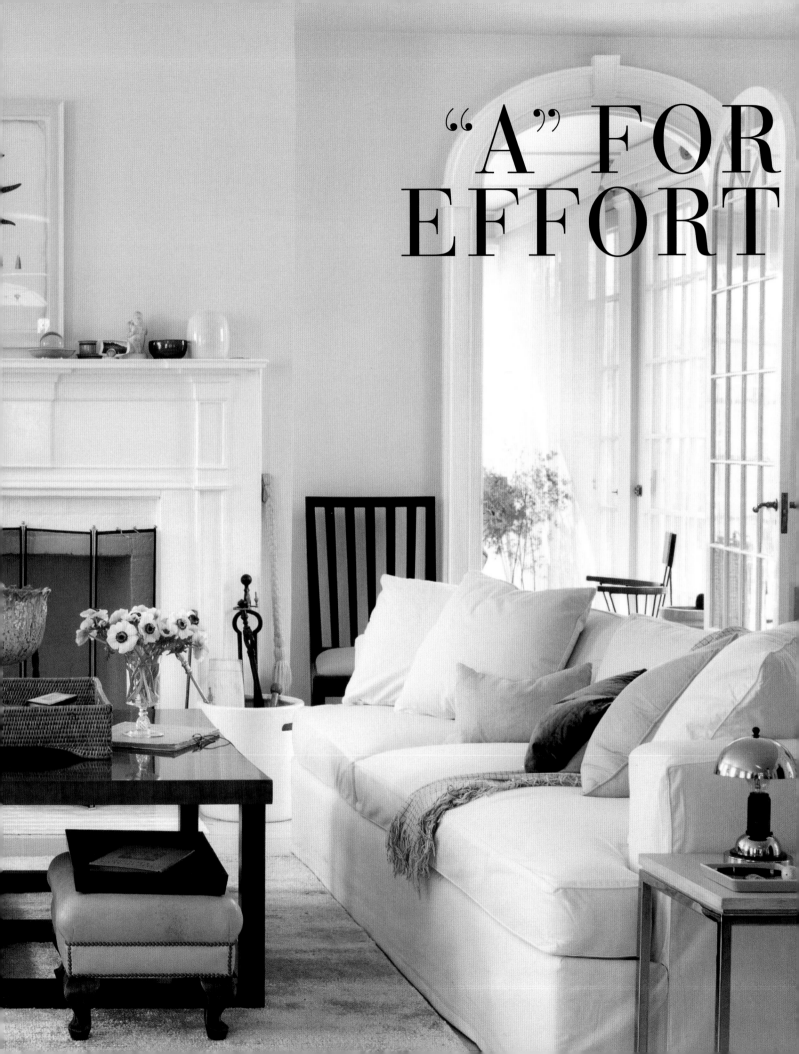

"A" FOR
EFFORT

W HEN THOMAS O'BRIEN OPENED THE glamorous, mercury-mirrored doors of Aero Studios in Manhattan's SoHo in 1992, the design firm and furniture gallery became a style maker overnight. Aero's artful assemblage of classic, vintage modern, and exotic furnishings, everyday found objects and casual accessories conjured an atmosphere of spare sophistication and easy luxury. It seemed a revelation. An A-list roster of clients swiftly followed, among them Ralph Lauren (O'Brien's former employer) and Giorgio Armani. O'Brien quickly moved into product and hotel design as well, collaborating with companies including Waterworks, Hickory Chair, Reed & Barton, Target and the Manhattan boutique hotel 60 Thompson, SoHo.

How does one acquire such winning and original style? It's likely that O'Brien was born with it. (Boyish good looks also happen to be part of his genetic equation.) But it helps to know that since he was very young, O'Brien has been an inveterate, indefatigable antiquer. Which may well explain the obsession with detail in his interior design work. He loves to carry a project through right down to the homey accessories, for instance, shopping for a mix-and-matchy holiday dinner service composed of rare Victorian soup plates, Edwardian blue-and-gold Wedgwood bone china and Early

While renovating, O'Brien somewhat ruefully ripped apart the house's decrepit kitchen in order to enlarge it. But the new space evokes the old, thanks to the designer's ingenious use of vintage-looking hardware and lighting, a bleached-cork floor and *bianco miele* marble.

American etched crystal goblets. "He won't settle," says Barbara Janulis, whose Colonial Revival house in Connecticut and an apartment on Fifth Avenue in New York have been restored and furnished by O'Brien. "When Thomas decorated my place in Connecticut for the Christmas season, he spent an hour just arranging the mantel. He found the perfect Victorian sleigh ornament for the centerpiece—it looked straight out of a Currier & Ives Christmas card," she marvels.

O'Brien began "going junking" as a boy with his father and grandmother in his native upstate New York. He thrilled to the hunt for objects with distinctive features—an early desk lamp with a graceful neck, a deerskin-covered ottoman—and displayed a knack for transforming derelict pieces into things freshly elegant by using unexpected upholstery or a dab of paint. But what he delighted in more than most were the narratives behind things: the table passed down through a family, or the delicately painted porcelain plates from the grandest house in town. Whether these items were precious or humble never concerned him. O'Brien's eye for beauty and his taste for a good story were all-encompassing. ("When I work with clients, I may equally recommend an object worth $40 or $40,000," he says.) Of course, like all great antiquers, he possesses a knack for being in exactly the right place at the right time—in other words, serendipity in abundance.

His discovery of the Academy, his five-bedroom house in Bellport, on Long Island's South Shore, was nothing if not serendipitous. For more than ten years, the Manhattan-based O'Brien would bicycle from his weekend cottage in neighboring Brookhaven through that charming, hedge-rimmed hamlet of Colonial-Revival homes on his way to the beach. (As befits O'Brien's low-key character, Bellport is the discreet summer retreat of such privacy-loving New Yorkers as Isabella Rossellini and Charlie Rose.) One day in the spring of 2001 he took a different route and came upon a nobly proportioned neoclassical-revival building—a library? a school? a private house?—in the early stages of decay. Closer inspection revealed exceptional details: an Adam-style fanlight, dentil moldings, arched doorways, a bell tower and, best of all, empty rooms. The house was for sale.

O'Brien has been in love with clean-lined neoclassicism since childhood, and almost instinctively he found himself heading for the realtor's office advertised on the sign in the front yard. A deal was struck without much trouble. And during the next two years, he reconceived, renovated and furnished the house with his signature celerity and skill. (The fact that one of his old friends, Randy Polumbo, happened to be a builder with New York's 3-D Laboratory also proved serendipitous.) In short order, the Academy

OVERLEAF: O'Brien combined several rooms to create a master suite; the corner bedroom still has its original fireplace.

RIGHT: In the master bath, O'Brien designed a vanity with the rugged grace of a piece of farmhouse furniture.

has become a showcase for O'Brien's lifetime of stylish scavenging. But more than simply a gracious home, it is also—this restless arranger can't help himself—a design lab, a place to try out new ideas and to tutor clients in his relaxed but ever-so-refined approach to living.

As its name suggests, the Academy began life in 1833 as a schoolhouse, Bellport's first. It played that role until 1902, when it became briefly a cabinetmaker's shop and then a private residence. The couple who bought it from the cabinetmaker moved it down the lane onto a two-acre lot, adding a wing with a kitchen below and bedrooms above, along with an entry portico and an enchanting enclosed porch with its own hearth. The wife, a poet, was so pleased with her new house that she versified its charms; O'Brien has made it his mission to preserve and update the poems. Along the way, he's clearly grown infatuated. What started out as a weekend house has become O'Brien's domestic anchor, a cherished retreat and a favored place for entertaining friends.

The designer is known for the convivial logic of his interiors, and his skill is apparent as soon as you walk into the great room, the Academy's former classroom. The high-ceilinged space has been divided into four seating areas that serve different functions and afford varying degrees of intimacy. The great room is painted a brilliant, glossy cool white from floor to ceiling, with many of its furnishings white or neutral, so that it glistens invitingly in daylight and glows, lanternlike, by night. The doors and stair rails are painted a glossy black, for a look O'Brien has archly termed "institutional romantic." (He was inspired, he says, by the lacquered walls of English public schools and the below-stairs rooms of the country house in the film *Gosford Park*. He's even furnished the Academy's bedroom windows with scholastic white pull shades; characteristically drab, they look swank here.)

Central to the great room and dividing it into two sections is an elegant pair of dining tables designed by O'Brien, vaguely fifties in style, with gray wooden tops and taut steel bases. Their stretchers meet to form an ellipse, a shape that reappears throughout the room—in the fanlight above the entry, in the arched doorways by the fireplace and indeed in many of the arranged objects. Such refined detailing is an O'Brien trademark. So, too, is the graceful counterpoint of straight lines and curves, textures and tones, and, most notably, period and modernist furniture that he's orchestrated. Take his collection of dining chairs, for instance. Most are tubular chrome pieces from the thirties, but O'Brien has mussed with their machine aesthetic by covering their back panels in pale pigskin and their seats in calf hair to soften their

O'Brien (left) was inspired by the crisp neoclassicism of his 1833 house.

appearance. At the tables' ends, he's placed a pair of slat-backed Georgian-style chairs in mahogany, part of the furniture line he designs for Hickory Chair. Severely linear and emphatically dark, especially against their pale surroundings, they almost look modern—in fact, O'Brien has modulated their proportions to contemporize their appearance. The designer calls the effect of this blending and transmuting of elements "warm modernism," and the results are so pleasurable you can barely detect the rigor behind them. It seems he can't help finessing details that will make all his favorite pieces get along, no matter what their generation or background.

Now that he's settled in at the Academy, O'Brien has begun inviting clients over for a look. Sharing lunch, they get to see how he sets a table with vintage china and silver, how he's grouped his collections of books around the rooms. On a tour of the second floor, they catch a glimpse of how he makes a bed with antique linens; they inspect his careful combination of several of the old bedrooms (there were seven when he bought the house; now there are five) to create a master suite, made up of a study, bedroom, large bath and dressing room. He talks to them about respecting the history of a house by recycling architectural features wherever possible, as he did here by using the old cabinet doors from the kitchen and bath in his newly built dressing room.

If the Academy is about style, it is also clearly about sentiment. It's now become home to many of O'Brien's favorite things, including his lunar and celestial maps, old prints of Manhattan, works by artist friends. One of the four guest rooms features a delicate antique bed he purchased and painted dark green when he was only twelve. Another is furnished with a beautifully carved 19th-century four-poster that was his grandmother's; a version of it will soon be introduced by Hickory Chair.

In the upstairs hallway, O'Brien points out what appears to be an old skylight. In fact, it's a window the designer installed to reveal a view of the handsomely beamed attic and the school bell tower above—a bit of the past wittily reframed for the present. In a glimpse, it seems to capture what O'Brien's stylish magic is all about.

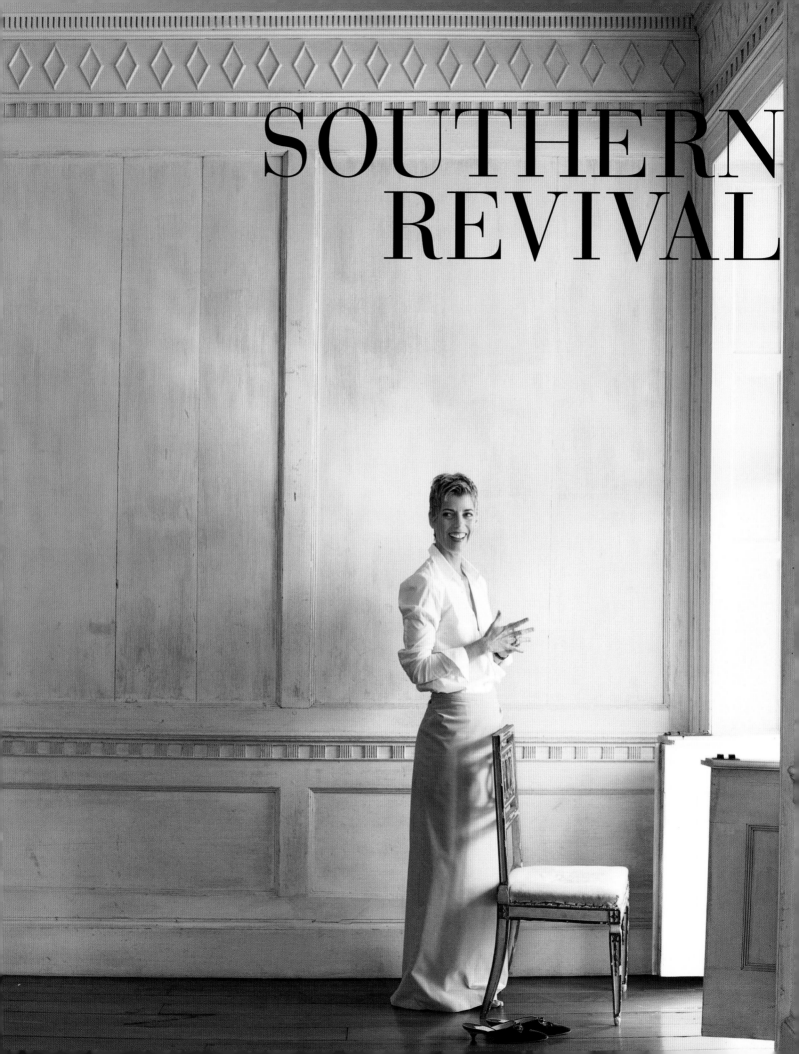

SOUTHERN REVIVAL

M OST PEOPLE, WHEN THEY close on a house in need of renovation, can't wheel in the Dumpster fast enough. They want the dining room to be a library, the library to be a home theater and the attic to be a spa—immediately, before another season races by. Not so Peter and Suzanne Pollak.

Back in 1996, the Pollaks were a couple with four teen-age children, whose housing needs were being fairly well met by a four-bedroom contemporary on Hilton Head Island, South Caro-lina. But a few times a year they liked to drive over the causeway to sleepy Beaufort, cruise past the Chocolate Tree candy store and the mansion where *The Big Chill* was filmed, and window-shop for houses. One day, caving in to impulse, they bought one. It was a modest but undeniably high-style Georgian dowager that had been standing on a bosky side street for more than 209 years, the last three of them with a For Sale sign out front. And the more the Pollaks learned of its traumatic history—which had included stints as a hospital during the Civil War, a kindergarten in the 1950s and an apartment building in the '60s and '70s—the more they came to believe that the house finally deserved a say in its own future.

No spa, in other words. No home theater. In this renovation, the owners, not the house, would be the ones to make the major life changes.

A circa 1915 portrait by George Luks hangs above a Chippendale mahogany bureau. The printed-cotton drapery fabric is from Geoffrey Bennison.

"I told Peter that buying it would be like having triplets—far too much work," recalls Suzanne Pollak. "He disagreed." It was a lot of work, of course. But Peter Pollak was focused on returning the house to the condition it might have been in had it remained in one family up to the present day. "Lived in, without looking like a museum," he explains.

The place had been built in 1780 for Carolina-born Elizabeth Barnwell Gough by her brother, with money from her father's estate. The house passed to her daughter, who brought up eleven children there. During its service as a Union army hospital, doors were taken off their hinges and used as stretchers—one of the countless indignities the house has endured, according to Suzanne. "This is really the first time it's been outfitted the way it was supposed to be," she says with a measure of pride.

No question the Pollaks have become converts to the old-house philosophy. "Living here is like therapy," Peter declares. "Do you know there are just eight rooms—and eight fireplaces? The closets are so small you realize you don't need about ninety percent of your clothes."

The dowager has benefited from their reverential attitude. Its exterior walls, made of tabby, an exceedingly rare composite of lime, sand and oyster shell, have now been patched and lime-washed to a delicate gray-green. The original ballroom paneling has been restored and glazed to complement the southern heart-pine floors; sculptural wing chairs and a ball-and-claw-footed table rest lightly on biscuit-colored Turkish carpets. For all its recovered dignity, though, the house possesses a casual air that flows out of the couple's enlightened interest not in copying the past, exactly, but in holding on to elements they consider functional and beautiful today.

"Suzanne thinks I must have lived here in another life," scoffs Peter, who can't quite hide his amusement at the idea. "How else would you explain it?" she counters. "Before we bought this place, Peter couldn't have cared less about historic houses or furniture. He must have lived here at least once—maybe it's been twice."

The house has boarded its share of old souls, including a couple of Civil War veterans whom the Pollaks went so far as to exorcise before they moved in (the ghosts were frightening the painters). Then again, Suzanne has a romantic imagination that's found a prodigious outlet in Beaufort, with its Walker Evans streetscapes and Spanish moss curtaining the trees like Scarlett O'Hara's iconic draperies.

"Beaufort has an amazing aura," she says in a resonant voice that seems outsized for her willowy figure. "In a way, I feel transported to another world here, another time." For most people this would be a disconcerting departure from

In the cypress-paneled parlor, a New England Federal wing chair and a Philadelphia Chippendale tea table—whose twin is in New York's Metropolitan Museum of Art—are both from G.K.S. Bush Antiques.

reality, but for Suzanne it's simply how things have always been. Born in Beirut to an American CIA man and his wife, she and her younger sister and brother were raised in Libya, Somalia, Nigeria, Ghana, Liberia—"all the hot spots," she says blithely. "Growing up, we moved every two years. If we didn't have a party instantly, then we never met anyone." Learning to put together a house and throw a party were Suzanne's ways of coming to terms with the constant dislocation, and they're skills she has never renounced.

Peter, a gregarious, sandy-haired Southerner Suzanne met at the University of Virginia, is president of DPS Sporting Club Development Company, LLC, whose real estate involvements (the Greenbrier sporting club, the Ford Plantation, Turks & Caicos Sporting Club, and others) reveal an appreciation of history and a talent for turning places that fire the imagination into moneymaking enterprises. Though he may not have lived in Beaufort before, he definitely grasps its appeal.

"This town used to be a great cotton port and a center for smuggling, too," he says with a nascent smile. "Now part of the town is on the National Register of Historic Places. To me, it's an absolutely elegant Southern coastal setting that still has a quiet, small-town feel. And I'm at a stage in my life right now when I appreciate quietness—because I can make a lot of noise."

Noise is just what the Pollaks' neighbors expected when the work began, but they were pleasantly surprised. The restoration turned out to be, in large part, a handcrafted labor of love.

Though Beaufort's historic status meant that aspects of the project would be dictated by the town's architectural review board, the Pollaks weren't fazed. They intended to do things right, and time wasn't really an issue—they would live in Hilton Head until their house was ready. (The entire project took eighteen months.) The previous owners had done quite a bit of thoughtful work during their twenty-year tenure, notably reassembling the interior, which had been divvied up into five apartments for several decades. They had reinstated the original layout of four rooms on the first floor and four on the second and added a kitchen to the rear facade (the original kitchen had been in an outbuilding). But the addition needed a lot of help—"It looked like an Esso gas station," cracks Suzanne—the second floor was virtually untouched, and the house hadn't been painted in nearly a century.

"From my work experience, I realized the house needed people at the top of their professions," says Peter, who oversaw the project and became obsessed with tracking down the appropriate craftsman for each aspect of the job. "It's not as expensive as one would think," he notes of the approach, "and you only have to do things

In the Pollaks' front hall, a New England Federal side chair rests beside an important circa 1810 Baltimore Federal pier table.

once." The process was not unlike an ongoing open house, with the Pollaks standing at the center holding the hors d'oeuvres. From Charlottesville came architect Jay Dalgliesh, noted for his historical restorations. From Hilton Head came contractors Cambridge Building Corporation. Color consultants Donald Kaufman and Taffy Dahl helped with the interiors, as did Suzanne's sister Cynthia Carter, an interior designer, and Guy Bush, a top dealer in American antiques. Advising on landscaping and exterior lighting were George S. Betsill, known for his work at the Greenbrier, and Susan Murray, of Palm Beach Lighting. Then there were the myriad contributions of dealers in old window glass, cast-iron doorstops and gas lighting, among others.

But before they could indulge in such details, the Pollaks had to oversee months of work on the facade. Dalgliesh supervised repairs to the roof, the gutters and the colonnaded front portico, all of which fell under the jurisdiction of the town's review board. A local craftsman set to work patching the exterior walls. To the Pollaks' horror, however, the surface started flaking off within a year. Enter Benjamin Wilson of Charleston, perhaps the nation's only building conservator who has thoroughly researched the esoteric construction material known as tabby.

According to the young preservationist, who speaks with all the fervor of a genome researcher, only about six tabby houses are still occupied today, and they are all on the southeastern seaboard, where oyster shells, lime and sand would have been plentiful more than two centuries ago. Wilson was thrilled to be entrusted with the Pollak house, and moved quickly to prescribe a cure for its ills.

"From the 1920s on, repairs had been made to the exterior of the house using concrete—which is harder, dries faster and lasts longer than tabby," he explains. "The Pollaks' first contractor used the wrong material for patching—it was as hard as china, and the building was absolutely shedding it like a skin. I removed it, along with the concrete, all the way up to the water table. Then we made patches with a putty of lime, sand and shells I made myself and restuccoed the facade. We let it cure, then we lime-washed it."

There were no regulations governing the house beyond the facade, but even so the Pollaks wanted the interior to relate closely to the exterior. Their plan was to hold on to whatever interior architecture and woodwork they could and to fill the house with a mix of the Federal-period antiques that might have been there in its youth.

They ordered handblown glass from Germany so that the windows would recover the watery beauty of the 18th-century originals, and had new Charleston-style shutters custom-made. In keeping with their plan to make the house livable rather than museumlike, they installed central heat and air and turned the full basement into a bunkhouse hangout for their three sons (their daughter's bedroom is upstairs).

One of Suzanne's best memories from that time is of working with color consultants Donald Kaufman and Taffy Dahl, who advised on finishes for the entire house. Their work was critical in establishing the enlightened historical approach that the Pollaks went on to apply to the interior.

According to Kaufman, "If you take the purely historical approach to color, you run into a quagmire of questions, because you really can't re-create a historically accurate color anymore—the materials are unavailable." A wiser approach, he says, is to adopt a historical intention.

All told, painting and refinishing took six months—not as long as the furnishing, which is still a work in progress. But that's what happens when you get hooked on Early American furniture and are befriended by your dealer, who always has the best interests of your growing collection in mind. "Peter and Suzanne are more fun than you can imagine," says Guy Bush, who met the couple when they appeared one day at his shop in the Georgetown neighborhood of Washington, D.C. "They have the same level of interest and energy—so rare in my experience. Usually it's the husband or the wife who is passionate."

Interspersed with the antiques are a few upholstered pieces the couple picked with the help of Cynthia Carter, who chose upholstery forms that would marry well with Federal silhouettes and still be comfortable as well as durable. (One of Peter's collecting principles is "Don't buy something you're afraid to sit on," and it takes only one look at his sons, who are all over six foot six, to appreciate his viewpoint.) Four years after giving in to temptation, the Pollaks admit that their Georgian dowager has indeed had her say. They are proud experts on 18th-century masonry techniques, reproduction lighting, historical paint color and Federal furniture, and they can't pass a hardware store without going in. "We have all these new interests we can share," says Suzanne. "It's strengthened our marriage."

Maybe more of us should consider listening to our houses?

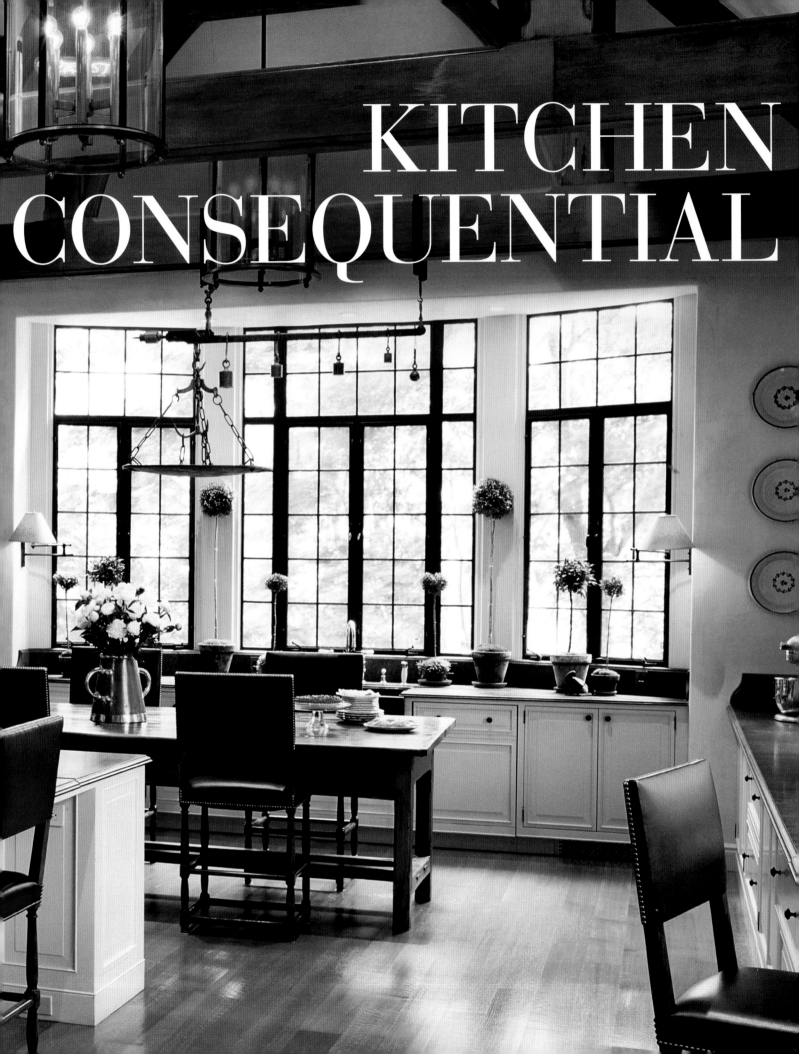

KITCHEN CONSEQUENTIAL

THERE WAS A TIME WHEN FAMILY LIFE revolved around the living-room fireplace. In most households these days, the domestic focus has shifted to the kitchen, where the feeling of warmth is generated not just by the gleaming stainless-steel stove sitting center stage. We Americans love our kitchens. And the bulk of kitchen remodeling spending goes toward what the industry considers high-end renovations, which means we're outfitting our kitchens with all the latest accoutrements: glass-fronted refrigerator-freezers worthy of professional chefs; drawers that can wash dishes, keep food warm or chill bottles of water, soda and wine; walk-in pantries as capacious as your average gourmet deli. The kitchens themselves are now bigger, too, in the hope that the family will gather—and reconnect—in one room. So new kitchens are being designed to accommodate the home office and homework; cozy conversing and solo Internet surfing; quiet checkbook balancing and watching a ball game with the gang (preferably on a high-definition flat-screen TV); and sometimes even eating a healthy meal or a hasty snack.

The fact of the matter, ironically, is that many people now find food preparation and consumption the least important aspect of their dramatic new multifunctional spaces. One much-loved and

much-cooked-in exception to this rule is a kitchen designed by Victoria Hagan as a seamless and very necessary addition to a stately 1940s stone manor house in Connecticut. The New York–based Hagan, known for her lyrical interpretations of classic American style, had worked with the owner, Colleen Hempleman, on several other projects. Indeed, Hempleman and her husband were two of Hagan's first clients when, as a twenty-two-year-old recent graduate of Parsons School of Design, she launched her own firm in the mid-1980s. So she knew their priorities well, and one thing Colleen Hempleman has always prioritized is cooking wonderful meals for her family.

When the Hemplemans and their two sons, now grown, moved from Westchester County, New York, into their current home in the mid-1990s, the kitchen was relatively small; years before, it had been converted from its initial purpose as a butler's pantry that was connected by a dumbwaiter to the kitchen proper in the basement. A redesign of this existing kitchen, no matter how clever, would never have been successful given its limited square footage. Returning to the original configuration, with the kitchen in the basement, might have worked in a bygone age when a staff prepared meals and entertaining was formal and firmly fixed in the dining room, but it would have been completely inadequate for a modern American family, like the

Hemplemans. And an early idea to convert a billiards room near the dining room was scrapped when they realized, to their surprise, that it was one of their favorite gathering places.

Since the house was otherwise in good structural shape, Hagan embarked on an extensive redecoration but left the crowbars and sledgehammers back at the office. "Rather than solve the kitchen problem immediately," Hempleman explains, "we decided that we would live here for a few years and figure out how we really wanted to use the house." Patience had its payoff, as it often does for home renovators. "Finally, we came to the decision that in order to get Colleen a full working family kitchen, we were going to have to add on," Hagan says.

The challenge was to design the twenty-by-thirty-two-foot addition for the new kitchen so that it appeared, from both the inside and the outside, as if it had always been a part of the house. First, Hagan chose to situate it right off the existing kitchen (which has become a pantry once again). Then traditional materials were chosen that related to those in the rest of the house: quartersawn oak floors; warm, richly grained, honed Pietra Cardoza stone countertops; a series of rugged wood trusses overhead; soft plaster walls; and metal casement windows that brought in lots of light and matched the home's originals.

Inspired though she may have been by the

Interior designer Victoria Hagan mixed materials to diversify the look of the large kitchen.

19th- and early-20th-century kitchens of English architect Edwin Lutyens, Hagan explains that the Hemplemans "couldn't ask for a more contemporary American kitchen," because of its use of up-to-the-minute technology and its highly efficient layout. (Hagan has designed so many kitchens at this point in her career, she considers herself something of an expert in the field; see page 218–221 for her practical advice.) "It's not only a highly functional kitchen but a versatile family room," she adds. "There's always a ton of activity going on. When the boys are home, you'll find them eating breakfast at the counter or reading the paper. Most of the family dinners are served at the antique farm table, where Colleen and her husband also entertain for upwards of ten friends. Colleen even has an area for concentrating

on her charity work." (Hempleman is a prominent supporter of, among other organizations, the American Red Cross.) One thing you won't find is a television, Hagan says. "This is a room centered on the joys of gathering around a table and sharing life's experiences over a great meal."

When she first sat down with Hagan to draft her wish list, Hempleman placed a custom-commissioned Bonnet stove at the top. Manufactured in France by a company that specializes in commercial appliances, the eleven-and-a-half-foot-long unit, with its handsome copper-and-brass hood, is very much the heart of the kitchen. (Home models range from $20,000 to more than $100,000.) Hagan and Hempleman talked to such experts as chef Gray Kunz, then cooking on a Bonnet at New York's four-starred Lespinasse, before settling on a particular set of attributes: a salamander for broiling and last-minute browning, a built-in bain-marie for keeping delicate sauces warm, a plancha for searing fish and steaks, four burners, an induction unit for making stews and melting chocolate, and "the most fabulous gas oven," according to Hem-pleman. "It gives off an incredibly reliable, steady heat because of its cast-iron lining." (Nearby are two additional built-in electric wall ovens, which Hempleman uses for baking pastries.)

Much as a living room's furniture layout often starts with the location and scale of the fireplace, Hagan explains, "this kitchen really developed around the Bonnet range. Its dimensions dictated the size of the island, and then we needed space for pantry storage and a full refrigerator and separate freezer at one end of the room, and at the other, the width to seat at least ten people around a great old farmhouse table." The table is six inches higher than the norm, so it can double as an additional work surface. An island provides even more counter space (another must-have on Hempleman's list) and has side-by-side sinks, allowing two people to work simultaneously, and twin dishwashers, which are fairly standard, says Hagan, in today's kitchens.

Although the room is quite spacious, the work triangle—kitchen-speak for the nexus of sink, stove and refrigerator—is fairly compact, which minimizes the amount of walking required while preparing a meal. There are also separate zones for baking and, beneath the kitchen's far wall of windows, flower arranging. (This area has a garden-view sink, used for supplementary cleanup when the Hemplemans host large parties.)

"If a room doesn't function well," Hagan says, "I don't care what it looks like." Happily, this room doesn't just function extraordinarily well; it's also exceptionally beautiful to look at. "We mixed materials and finishes, which a lot of people are reluctant to attempt. But given the scale of the room, we thought that we could pull it off." So amid the ivory-colored cabinetry (a shade Hagan calls "creamy, almost scrimshaw white") are accents of natural wood that have been treated with a limed finish to complement the white-and-blue delft plates hung on the walls. Meanwhile, the stone counters harmonize with vintage terra-cotta tiles behind the stove, burnished wood floors and ceiling trusses and, perhaps most dramatically, an extensive collection of antique copper pots (some of which Hempleman actually uses on a daily basis). All is suffused with a warm light, derived from the room's three exposures and electrical illumination from various sources: highly directed recessed ceiling lights, under-cabinet lights, sconces at the windows and general illumination provided by a trio of Poillerat lanterns (only one is an antique; Hagan commissioned two modern-day copies).

"Kitchen design is about the details," Hagan admits. It's also about something inchoate, difficult to pin down, that usually begins—and ends—with the client. "Colleen sees cooking as an enhancement of her love of family, home and sharing. People often ask me what's the most important quality of my projects, and I always say that they can't just be stage sets. They need to be honest and a reflection of the people who live there." The designer pauses and adds: "Colleen's kitchen certainly qualifies in that regard. It has not only got great character; it's got real soul."

DESIGN FORUM
CRAFTING A COOK'S KITCHEN

Architect James D'Auria gave Frank and Barbara Sciame an expansive breakfast room adjacent to both kitchen and sitting rooms.

If you have more than one kitchen, perhaps one in the city and one in the country, which do you prefer? Chances are it's the country kitchen.

Because they offer so many opportunities for expansion, personalization and, let's face it, self-indulgence, country kitchens often become everyone's favorite room in a second home. With a sizeable kitchen, located just off a screen porch or mudroom and on the way to the bedrooms, a living room may well become obsolete—or at least a much quieter place. Planning this kind of room begins with a thoughtful assessment of the house as a stylistic whole. Even the most formal of architectural statements—Greek Revival, Italianate, Georgian—can be receptive to a large and welcoming kitchen, as long as the dimensions aren't so sprawling that the kitchen threatens to overwhelm the surrounding spaces. In a more relaxed building type—Victorian, Dutch Colonial, shingle, bungalow, ranch—rooms can flow more easily into one another and such divisions aren't an issue.

CASE STUDY: A KITCHEN RENOVATION

When Frank and Barbara Sciame set about renovating their house in coastal Connecticut, previously the longtime weekend home of Katharine Hepburn, they decided to move the cramped, dark kitchen from one end of the 8,000-square-foot English-style cottage right into the center of the layout, where it's now flanked on the south side by the entry hall and on the north by the living room. To the east, through a framed opening, lies a breakfast room that manages to seem both open to the kitchen action and set slightly apart, where the couple can read the newspaper on Sunday mornings with an unimpeded view of Long Island Sound.

Though the house, constructed in 1939 on the site of a shingle-style cottage lost to a hurricane, was originally designed without much interior detailing, architect James D'Auria added what he felt would be appropriate to a residence of its size and age. In the kitchen, that meant

The Sciames' new kitchen has a vintage character, thanks to beadboard cabinetry and Carrera marble for the double sink and countertops.

distinctive and harmonious choices that look back to the English character of the architecture: beadboard cabinetry, marble countertops, a roomy stone farmhouse sink, a blue Aga stove and a hanging plate rack for Barbara's collection of blue-and-white china.

CREATING VIEWS, INSIDE AND OUT

When an extraordinary natural landscape beckons right outside the kitchen window, it's crucial to bring that view into the room. Here are some ways to make that happen.

■ Choose your window type to complement the architectural style of the house. It might be a traditional window seat, modern sliding glass doors, or even hacienda-style small-paned windows—likely the choice will already be in use elsewhere on the house. Musician Lindsay Buckingham and his wife, Kristen, chose small-paned kitchen windows for their Bel Air hilltop retreat. The couple worked with designer Madeline Stuart on a Mediterranean-style kitchen outfitted with ceramic-tile floors and rustic ironwork.

■ If you're building a kitchen addition, consider the building orientation very carefully. East-facing views can be especially intoxicating in kitchens because they access the day's first light; west-facing views are spectacular at day's end. When do you spend the most time in your kitchen?

■ The view from a screen porch epitomizes the rural residential experience for many Americans. Why not create a screen porch off the kitchen? The rudimentary structure adapts surprisingly well to many building styles. In Water Mill, New York, architect Steven Holl designed a contemporary cedar-clad house for Joan and Martin Camins with an east-facing kitchen wall that opens onto a small screen porch. The simple palette of materials Holl marshaled for use in the kitchen—subtly tinted concrete floors and countertops, white oak cabinets, stainless steel appliances—transition well into the rest of the rigorously designed house.

ABOVE: *In Eva Lorenzotti's New York kitchen, a mix of materials keeps things interesting: granite for counters, zinc on the table, cabinets of wood and fritted glass.*

LEFT: *Eastern light beams through a shallow screen porch into the kitchen of Joan and Martin Camins. Architect Steven Holl saw the porch's potential to double as a breakfast room.*

217

In Amagansett, New York, architect James D'Auria designed a barnlike house for his family that embraces a stone terrace.

■ Once your kitchen grows to a certain size, as it inevitably will in a second home, it's time to start thinking about creating interior views that will entertain the eye. Decorator Thomas Jayne did this beautifully in a plantation-style house on the Georgia coast, where the traditional low-country kitchen featured sage-colored beadboard and other period details. To lighten the mood, Jayne chose a 1962 dining table by Florence Knoll and hung a bright mobile over it. Visible from the kitchen, the combination amounts to a visual smile.

■ Aim for interior views that reinforce the architectural character of the space. Designer Thomas O'Brien's own kitchen in Bellport, on the south coast of Long Island, features details that signal the building's past as a turn-of-the-century schoolhouse. A bold clock face reminds cooks to check the time, or risk burning the main course; industrial-style lights over the marble-topped island have a no-nonsense air that suits pastry-making and other kitchen arts. "It's old-world design used in a modern way," says O'Brien, who is known for such inspired mixing.

Given all the stylistic fantasies a kitchen in the country can fulfill, it's important to remember that at the end of the day it must be functional, too. You might be surprised to find yourself hosting a wedding reception, a retirement party, a christening picnic or a college reunion barbecue one day, events a city kitchen might not be called on to accommodate.

THE KITCHEN WE ALL WANT

The rudiments of kitchen design are ones interior designers study most diligently, and their expertise is worth having. New York–based Victoria Hagan, whose clients frequently bring her in to help with their second homes in places like Aspen, Telluride and the Hamptons, likens it to solving a puzzle. Hagan notes that there are several tricks of the trade she always applies—and readily shares.

Inside, the casual D'Auria cook space measures twenty-five feet square—which is ideal for cooking and entertaining simultaneously.

No matter what the size of the room, keep the work triangle tight. Minimize the distance between the sink, stove and refrigerator (and garbage disposal, best located next to the sink) to save your legs and feet.

Good lighting is critical. "Generally I mix halogen and incandescent bulbs," she explains, "and I recommend three sources: under-cabinet lighting, direct lighting from a source in the ceiling for specific tasks and then a general and more decorative source, like a pendant fixture."

Don't be timid about mixing things up. Different materials and finishes can be more interesting than a classic-but-safe kitchen, and that's especially pertinent in a casual and part-time room.

Finally, don't obsess over current trends—or design advice, for that matter. "Ultimately," says Hagan, "it's about whatever works for you." That's a sentiment that should apply to other rooms in the house beyond the kitchen—so cut it out and pin it . . . to the refrigerator.

ABOVE: *Victoria Hagan's favorite kitchen layout: a corridor of appliances and an island facing a roomy seating area.*

LEFT: *The Buckingham family's Mediterranean-style kitchen in L.A. has west-facing views of the Pacific through leaded-glass windows.*

221

CHAPTER THREE
ARTFUL LIVING

M

AKING A HOME IS A CREATIVE ACT THAT BEGINS with the setting and style we choose—town or country, glass box, home on the range— and never really ends. For some of us, it's the journey of a lifetime. We build a garden, a library, an art collection that expresses who we are beyond words. For a few of us, it can even be the journey of several lifetimes, as we pass down the predisposition that leads a new generation into the arts. How our cultural interests come home is endlessly fascinating to *Town & Country*. The magazine has followed trendsetters and iconoclasts with equal interest, and the resulting stories all have something to tell us about the power of art to help us know ourselves.

For some of the magazine's subjects, living both in and with art is second nature. Manfredi della Gherardesca grew up in Tuscany between estates that have been in his family for generations. When he married and moved to London in the 1990s, Gherardesca and his wife bought a house and began making it their own from scratch. They commissioned the interiors from England's best young design talent, creating a remarkable envelope for their collection of contemporary art. By advancing the concept of patronage into his own time, Gherardesca is influencing a new generation.

Today's patrons continue to redraw the map of how art and life intersect. Gallery-like spaces and even freestanding buildings to house a collection are in vogue, and, following a thirty-year trough, the field of furniture design is hot again. Needless to say, some of the collectors featured on our pages have set the trend's wheels in motion.

A hallway in the Lignel town house holds Andy Warhol portraits of Freud and Kafka.

ART FORUM

OVERLEAF: Paris-based architect Jean-Michel Wilmotte designed most of the furniture in the Lignels' New York town house, including a desk and bookshelves in Jean's office.

RIGHT: Daphné Lignel, with daughters Tess and Margaux. Keith Haring's 1986 *Silence = Death* hangs above an Yves Klein gold-leaf and Plexiglas table.

I BEGAN MY FOURTH LIFE IN 1992," SAYS JEAN Lignel, who is sitting on the top floor of his family's town house, surrounded by his favorite paintings. The recently renovated house is tucked away on a leafy street in one of Manhattan's oldest downtown neighborhoods.

Lignel is the kind of man who reinvents himself every few years. In his case the process began in 1968, when he gave up his job as a schoolteacher and worked his way into the newspaper business in his native France, eventually buying several papers, including the Lyon-based *Le Progres*. In 1986 he divested himself of his publishing concerns and turned to international investing; the next big change, initiating his fourth life, as he explains it, came when he crossed paths with Daphné Pairaudeau, then a student at the Sorbonne, who is thirty years his junior.

"I met her at a dinner party in Paris on September 22, 1992, and asked her to marry me a week later," he says with a smile. (She waited several months before saying yes.)

The couple began spending time in New York, in an apartment Jean owned in Greenwich Village. Daphné took acting lessons, and Jean studied jazz piano at the New School and later jazz singing at the Manhattan School of Music. He now produces jazz recordings under his own label, Rosebud Music, and has established a

The dining area doubles as a gallery for paintings by Keith Haring, Andy Warhol and Chuck Close, interspersed with African masks and Han-dynasty figures.

small publishing house, la maison Red, which specializes in fine-art books.

Throughout all these changes, Jean's passion for art, now shared with Daphné, has provided continuity in a multifaceted life. He started collecting when he was only sixteen, his first acquisition a small pastel by Jerome Hart. His collection then expanded to include Impressionist and Old Master paintings and ancient clay figures from China and the Celebes islands. In 1979 he turned to Pop Art; more recently, the couple has focused on postwar and contemporary work.

The inveterate collectors are also lovers of houses. Daphné and Jean have a pied-à-terre off the Champs-Élysées in Paris and a farmhouse and vineyard in Beaujolais; they rent a summer place on the Riviera and an apartment in London, the family's primary residence. But their preferred roost is the Manhattan house that holds many of their art treasures.

Behind an unassuming 19th-century brick facade, the 6,680-square-foot building unfolds in a sequence of multilevel spaces. "The idea was to make a house for the paintings and for us," says Daphné, referring to the couple's four children: Margaux, nine; Tess, seven; Milo, five; and Diego, five months (Jean also has four grown children from a previous marriage: Mathieu, Karine, Benjamin and Baptiste).

The new structure was actually built on an odd-shaped, constricted site, where a carriage house and stables had originally stood. Manhattan-based architect Jeffrey Flanigan negotiated a daunting series of city codes and historic-landmark restrictions to make the new program work. His primary mission: to create a series of galleries for the Lignels' large-scaled painting and sculpture art while also making an environment for casual family living—a place where art and life could mingle without inhibition.

On a typical weekday afternoon, baby Diego and his paraphernalia occupy the floor beneath a group of Keith Haring paintings in the living room, while five-year-old Milo is eating cereal at the kitchen counter in front of a full-length self-portrait by Joseph Beuys. The girls are in the playroom, where work by Donald Baechler and others hangs alongside their own. In this private museum there is no separation, no velvet rope, between priceless artifacts and the stuff of everyday life.

Flanigan's first challenge was to bring natural light into the recesses of the three-story house, which he accomplished by inserting a glass-lined courtyard into the very core of the structure. All the rooms are wrapped around this central shaft, giving them an almost subaqueous glow. On the first floor are the entry foyer, living and dining areas and the kitchen. The second floor holds the children's bedrooms; the third

floor is reserved as the adult domain, comprising a master-bedroom suite, a media room, Jean's office and a private sunlit balcony. One entire wall of the bedroom is covered with nude studies by painter Ida Applebroog, which imbue the room with an erotic aura.

Connecting the various levels is a sculptural staircase cantilevered out from one wall and supported by a pair of slender steel fins; a light well on the roof adds a dramatic cast to one's ascent as light trickles down through steps of perforated steel.

Flanigan's second challenge was to integrate architecture and art so closely that one flows seamlessly into the other, each reinforcing the other's impact. During the early stages of the design process he made a computer model with miniatures of the principal pieces to be displayed. The internal logic of rooms and passageways was in large part predetermined by the collection—as is the case in the living room, whose ceiling soars upward for two floors to accommodate Keith Haring's *Silence = Death* (1986), a brash pink-and-silver elegy for victims of the AIDS epidemic.

Another massive Haring, on the opposite wall, depicts a pair of scissors cutting a cord, while a third shows two bubble-headed figures making love. The cartoon imagery is oddly in sync with the ancient and primitive pieces grouped elsewhere around the room. French architect Jean-Michel Wilmotte, a family friend, designed all the new furniture in the house. Echoing the minimalist restraint of the architecture, it was fabricated of pickled beechwood in Paris and then shipped to New York.

A clever Wilmotte-designed desk and shelving fill Jean's office, which is down a luminous corridor on the third floor. After the ultramodern expanse of the lower levels, this inner sanctum comes as a surprise. It feels intimate and reserved, almost like stepping back into 19th-century France. The shelves are filled with well-worn leather-bound volumes, and there are family photographs. A large Vuillard painting of a garden party hangs on one wall; a Renoir river scene and works by Bonnard and Boudin are nearby.

Sitting at his desk, among his most prized possessions, Jean grows pensive as he describes growing up in Paris and the influence his grandmother had on him. "She lived on the Quai Voltaire and taught me all about art," he recalls.

"I am happy here," he says, glancing up at the Vuillard, but the phone rings and breaks his reverie: it is his other life calling him back to the present. Daphné and baby Diego are down below, ready to be taken to lunch at Fleur de Sel, a restaurant on East 20th Street that is yet another pet project for Jean, a co-owner. He hurries down the stainless-steel stairway to fetch the car.

232

PERFECT PARIS PENTHOUSE

OVERLEAF: Giancarlo Giammetti put together his 6,500-square-foot Paris apartment with rigor and passion, adding antiques and paintings piece by piece. Here, a Cy Twombly in the reception room.

RIGHT: Francis Bacon's 1978 *Study for a Portrait* communes with a bronze armchair by Claude Lalanne.

G IANCARLO GIAMMETTI—VALENTINO Garavini's longtime partner, the business brain behind their fashion empire—knows all about living well. Strung together like the pearls on a family necklace, the duo's various separate homes— five for Valentino, four for Giammetti—include villas in Rome and Tuscany, a château in France, a chalet in Gstaad and apartments in New York, London, Rome and Paris, as well as the couturier's fabled 152-foot yacht, *T.M. Blue One*. Living large? Living glamorously? No one does it better.

This gilded lifestyle is defined with discrimination in Giammetti's Parisian penthouse atop a landmark 1930s Art Deco building on the Left Bank's Quai d'Orsay. Although he put the duplex together in 1996 with American architect Peter Marino, Giammetti shows it off with the proud enthusiasm of a new owner.

Overscaled bay windows on both floors reveal a stupendous panorama. Above trees and across the Seine, your eyes light on the glass roof of the Grand Palais on the Right Bank opposite, catch the gleam of the statues on the Pont Alexandre III and come to rest on the Gothic spires of the neighboring American Church.

The interiors are as stunning as the view. Like a floating comma, a swooping staircase of dark *ipé* wood and silvered bronze connects the two floors and marks the divide between the living and

dining spaces of the extended main room on the first floor. Blue-chip postwar and contemporary paintings demand your attention next: two Andy Warhol portraits of Lenin, one red, one black, dominate the dining area at one end of the room; at the other, a huge, untitled gray-and-white Cy Twombly is enthroned over the black marble fireplace and surrounded by floor-to-ceiling bookcases. In between, the curves of a dazzling Francis Bacon, *Study for a Portrait*, of George Dyer, echo those of the bay window opposite. Claude Lalanne's sinuous bronze crocodile chair sits beneath the Bacon, completing the vignette. Glamorous living indeed.

When Giammetti, stepping into the familiar role of charming Italian host, comes to greet you, it is truly evident that this spellbinding

apartment continues to be an accurate reflection of its impeccably turned-out owner. The colors—black, silver, gray—are his colors; the cool, cerebral perfection is his perfection. How he attained this perfection is a story that began in 1996, when he decided to look for a Parisian pied-à-terre. "I love having new houses," he confides as we speak in his reception room. "And I don't like living in a hotel. For a long time, I had been coming here at least four times a year for the shows, which last two or three weeks, so Paris was the right choice."

Acquiring the three apartments (two on the lower floor, another one and a maid's room on the top floor) that make up this three-bedroom duplex took a miraculously short six months. He then asked architect Marino, who had already done his penthouse in Rome, to take on the Paris project. Working together for a year and a half, they succeeded in unifying the components sumptuously and seamlessly.

Giammetti was fully involved in the decoration. "I am very clear with those who help me that I don't want a turnkey apartment, with everything ready-made, including the flowers," he explains. "All my homes are about my own style and taste, which I have developed over the years." The art collection here, which also includes a Rothko, a Modigliani bust and a fabulous Picasso upstairs in the study off Giammetti's bedroom, is a personal passion. The two Warhol

Lenins in the dining area were bought years apart, and he took great satisfaction in putting them together: "I like to have Warhols in several colors, because it was what Andy wanted at the beginning." The art on display evolves based on Giammetti's latest buy. The Warhol *Double Elvis* (showing the singer as a gunslinger) that once greeted guests like a double whammy at the top of the stairs has been relocated to his London flat, and a gray Rothko has taken its place. Warhol's *Hammer and Sickle* has superseded a red Twombly in the dining area, while *Great American Nude #93*, by Tom Wesselmann, a new acquisition, has yet to be hung.

Giammetti made finding the antiques for the apartment a joint effort with Marino. Because of the building's architecture, Art Deco was one of the periods they sought out. "I went everywhere," he says, "to Vallois, Anne-Sophie Duval, Jean-Jacques Dutko. Paris is still the best place to buy Art Deco." The results of this shopping spree—"beautiful lacquer and parchment tables by Emile-Jacques Ruhlmann, Jean-Michel Frank, Eileen Gray and Paul Dupré-Lafon"—are sprinkled around the living area. A drinks table by Eugène Printz sits under a Picasso drawing in a corner. A set of dining chairs by Ruhlmann, "made for a maharaja," adds Giammetti, surrounds two early-19th-century oval tables that Marino found in Stockholm.

And yet there is no slavish subservience to an Art Deco decor. "In a modern apartment you should mix," Giammetti affirms. "And I always like to mix with something very different." Here, his eclectic combinations fuse eye-popping avant-garde art with eye-popping antiques, like the glorious pair of 17th-century lacquer-and-bronze Japanese chests mounted on 18th-century gilt stands from *antiquaire* Didier Aaron.

For Marino, this project was something of a milestone. "It's an apartment people always remember, a real standout," he says proudly. "And it absolutely proves my theory that you can mix good contemporary architecture with antiques, modern paintings and modern textiles and still be comfortable. There is a big trend of thinking that once you are modern, you can't be comfortable—you can't have a sofa that you can relax on or have some of your heirlooms in the decor. Everything has to be so architectonic. I think that is a load of baloney, and this apartment has really made converts to good, clean modern taste." Along with the critical kudos, he emphasizes, "so many people say to me, 'That is exactly how I want to live.' It brought us a lot of work."

Giammetti and Valentino are famous in the fashion world for their lavish entertaining at home. Since acquiring this apartment, Giammetti has gained a base for the sophisticated soirées he likes to host. On those occasions a celebrity

is likely to be draped over every chair, and the chair will be a comfortable one indeed. Marino designed a plethora of soft seating throughout the vast reception room. He also created a sliding panel that can conceal the dining area during cocktails and then be opened up for added dinner-party pizzazz.

As Giammetti leads a tour of the apartment, dozens of details whisper absolute luxury. Still clearly delighted with the fine points after

Paris at his feet: the view from Giammetti's bedroom window encompasses the American Church next door and the Grand Palais across the Seine. *A fauteuil de page* awaits.

241

The gilt-bronze bed, from dealer Ariane Dandois in Paris, has a snakeskin-patterned spread woven by Le Manach. Beyond the bedroom lies the master study.

almost a decade, he calls attention to bookcases whose ebonized wood is inlaid with silver; to the master bath, a cloud of opaline glass the color of pale celadon; and to the dressing-room cupboards, cleverly hidden behind shagreen-patterned doors. "How nice not to have anything sticking out," he says. "I adore the way Peter works on the total look; the craftsmanship's so incredible. He calls this house a couture apartment."

In the master bedroom, the couture theme is carried through on the 19th-century Neapolitan gilt-bronze and wrought-iron bed, an antique not quite in its original form. Wanting an uninterrupted view of Paris (seen from here, the panorama is even more astonishing), Giammetti explains that he and Marino simply dropped the footboard of the bed to meet the floor. "Now it is a completely bastard bed destroyed by Mr. Giammetti," he says with a laugh.

"This is the perfect apartment for privacy," Marino sums up—"bedrooms upstairs and entertaining spaces downstairs, with great views from both floors." And the private rooms are as commodious as the public ones; the master suite is as large as the living room below. "So many apartments are disproportionate—the public rooms are huge and the private ones small. Here, they balance really well. I recommend that everyone buy three apartments," Marino quips. "It works so much better."

SWEET
AND LOW

TAKE A HIGH-PROFILE ITALIAN COUPLE with a desire for a low-key lifestyle. Add one of the brightest comets in the architectural firmament working today. Mix in a flat cornfield in the Veneto region of northern Italy, and come up with a surprising and striking 21st-century architectural gem.

The Invisible House—designed by Japanese architect Tadao Ando for Alessandro Benetton, merchant banker and vice chairman of his family's $2.1 billion conglomerate and fashion empire; his partner, Italian ski champion Deborah Compagnoni; and their two children—is as much a family residence as it is a masterful demonstration of Ando's seductive modernism.

The prominence of the players in this tale might lead one to expect a trophy house that dominates its setting. The reality is quite the opposite. The dwelling is deliberately concealed on a seven-and-a-half-acre property located in a coveted residential enclave near the city of Treviso. Instead of "Look at me," the game here is "Find me if you can." This architectural response exactly suited Benetton's succinct brief.

"I like a lot of privacy and a lot of light," he told Ando in 1999, when he engaged the Osaka-based Minimalist. "It is important that the architect have the right level of freedom," says the tall, handsome banker with amused green eyes. He's sitting

LEFT: The concrete walls of the house create a pared down backdrop for Benetton's art collection, which includes *L'Eventualità*, a 1964 work by Lucio Fontana.

RIGHT: Alessandro Benetton and Deborah Compagnoni's residence may be an extraordinary work of architecture, but above all it is a home for them and their children, Tobias and Agnese.

in the living room of the new house, where a massive black-and-white action painting by Lucio Fontana almost covers one wall. "You kind of have to give him guidance of what you need to have, but not too much," he continues. "Leave him to express himself."

The request was less modest than it may appear. "In reality, it was not an easy objective to achieve," Benetton explains. "We are in the flat Venetian countryside, with many houses around. At the beginning, I was a little bit questioning, wondering, 'Is he going to make it?' I closed my eyes and thought, 'If he promises a lot of light, he will do it.' And, definitely, I'd say he was very successful."

Privacy has also been assured, because it takes a drive into the heart of the property to see anything of the house at all. At the end of a gravel walk, Ando trumpets the entrance to the residence with a lofty twenty-one-foot-high rectangular box sheathed in gleaming Aluco-bond (an aluminum-finished cladding material). But the rest of the 13,000-square-foot building barely raises its concrete brow above the ground-level greenery. The architect's ingenious concept becomes apparent only from the back of the L-shaped structure, where the lawn swoops down some 120 feet to reveal the full elevation of the two-story modernist manor.

"I have explored an image of a house

connected to mother earth and corresponding to the surrounding environment," the architect has written of the design. In fact, a vast chunk of mother earth was excavated in order to situate the residence partly underground. The front and rear facades were carefully positioned to face southwest and northeast, taking maximum advantage of the sun in all seasons. The walls inside and out are the definition of Minimalist beauty. Made of cast concrete, which under Ando's touch has become a luxury material, they are a satin-smooth foil for the changing expressions of natural light that play such a vital role in his work.

As the project (which took two years to plan and two to build) progressed, Benetton had little doubt about the architectural outcome.

Veneto might be considered downright eccentric. Thousands of lovely Palladian villas dot the countryside, a legacy of the wealthy 16th- and 17th-century Venetians who traveled up the rivers in the summer, searching for cooler breezes. (One palazzo has been restored as the Benetton company headquarters, another as the premises for its cultural foundation.)

In fact, Benetton and Compagnoni were living in an apartment on the top floor of a Venetian villa in town when he decided to ask the architect to make some drawings for a house. At the time, Ando was working in Treviso on a major Benetton commission: Fabrica, the company's Communications Research Center (1992–2000).

"Architecture is in my family DNA," says Benetton. He grew up in a residence that his father, Luciano Benetton, cofounder of the family's empire, commissioned in the 1960s from the Italian architect Tobia Scarpa. Ando's dazzling Fabrica (which is also mainly underground) is a reaffirmation of the Benettons' avant-garde philosophy.

"For us, architecture is more than architecture; it is sort of a discovery of the future," Alessandro Benetton emphasizes. "We try to look for what comes next."

The Benetton house is Ando's largest private residence to date. The floor plan is rectangular and plain, but the architect is a virtuoso

"But I was scared that even though I liked this house very much, moving in would be difficult," he confesses. "Would it have the atmosphere of a nice warm house? Or would it be like a museum, just a beautiful building? The nicest surprise was that when we moved in, it was amazing, not just for me but for my family as well. It immediately felt like a nice warm house. It was home."

Almost on cue, Tobias, fresh from a swim, scampers across the room to jump into his father's arms. It's evident that the family is entirely at ease in this work of art.

If commissioning your own architectural showpiece is more daring than snapping up an already acclaimed house by, say, Richard Neutra or Frank Lloyd Wright, doing it here in the

at creating complex interiors from his simple plans. This translates into a mix of up and down, public and private—not conventional, perhaps, but producing beautiful spatial effects. The dramatic entrance passage at ground level leads, variously, to the guest suite and the foyer, and from the latter to the master-bedroom suite as well as to a bridge that spans a double-height living room below and links to the rooms of Tobias and his sister, Agnese ("Mimi"). Next door is a state-of-the-art gym; when Benetton makes it home in time to work out before dinner, the gym "becomes a playroom, too," he says, with the children bringing in their toys and joining him. The living room, dining room and kitchen quarters are on the floor below, which

Over the years, Ando intends that the house will become hidden among hundreds of trees, planted according to the architect's landscape scheme.

opens onto a courtyard, a terrace and greenery, so there is never a feeling of being underground.

Despite the size, there is nothing that looks too big or out of balance, not even the soaring living room, where Benetton is explaining just what it takes to be an architectural patron. Understanding how to respect Ando's sense of proportion was part of Benetton's learning curve. "There was no possibility of saying I wanted the entrance smaller because I didn't need it, or I wanted a certain room bigger because I needed more space there," he admits.

Although Ando had the final word on every detail of the project, the interior furnishings benefited from Compagnoni's relaxed, natural style. With help from Milan architect Piero Lissoni, she brought just the right touch of informality to the living room, adding three comfortable sofas of Lissoni's design to a scheme that also includes an iconic black leather Mies daybed and a glass table by Carlo Scarpa. Ando himself designed a simple trestle table that seats ten for the dining room.

Privacy and light, but also beauty and a rare sense of sanctuary, are the rewards of this architectural adventure. "I love the tranquillity," Compagnoni marvels. "The special thing about being here is that there are no pressures from outside—no noises, no voices and no chaos from the traffic or the town. Just birdsong."

253

STYLE
CENTRAL

OVERLEAF: A new statuary marble floor in the Krakoffs' kitchen makes a sleek foil for ostrich-covered Louis XV-style chairs by Jansen (left); Delphine and Lily by the pool on the four-acre property (right).

RIGHT: In the entry hall, a pair of John Dickinson lamps occupy a console table designed by the French artist Pierre Le-Tan.

VEN WHEN HE'S PADDING ABOUT barefoot and she's unwrapping charcuterie at their country house in Southampton, there's no mistaking that Delphine and Reed Krakoff are an "It" couple. It's not the cashmere-casual clothes they wear, requisite for any cool weekend in the Hamptons, nor the name-brand furnishings that populate their rooms. After all, she's an interior designer for the upper reaches of the Forbes 400, and he's the president and executive creative director of Coach, the leather-accessories-company-turned-fashion-icon.

No, beyond the pair's charisma and dual-career success lies something more. What emanates from these two, even on a Saturday morning, when most other couples with young children are wrangling over who gets to go to the gym or to yoga class first, is their seductive and full-time zeal for tapping into the most interesting trends in fine art and furniture.

Reed Krakoff takes his role as tastemaker seriously. According to James Zemaitis, the head of the 20th-century-design department at Sotheby's, Reed has had an extraordinary influence on other collectors by "hosting salons at his town house in New York, where he'll mix fashionistas with design-world dealers, and auction specialists, like me, with art-world denizens."

Delphine is the hostess at these lively affairs. And although she was born in Paris, together the Krakoffs epitomize the

OVERLEAF: Karl Springer python tables, a Louis XVI sofa and other treasures come to rest on a custom carpet by David Hicks Paris in the living room.

RIGHT: Reed Krakoff describes the master bedroom as an exercise in colorlessness. The painting over the mantel is by Christian Bérard.

all-American breed that thrives in cosmopolitan settings where work flows seamlessly into play. When at home in Manhattan, the couple keeps a busy schedule of social and business events: cochairing the Cooper-Hewitt National Design Awards; serving as honorary cochairs of the Winter Antiques Show; even stepping up to a dais to receive an award or two themselves. In 2004 Reed was named Accessory Designer of the Year for the second time by the Council of Fashion Designers of America, in recognition of his role as creative midwife for Coach's enormously profitable rebirth. In his years at the helm, Reed has ushered in a new golden age for the leather-goods maker. Revamping Coach's staid but sturdy burgundy-and-beige image with saucy, clean graphics and fashionable colors and honing a sixth sense for new trends in must-have accessories (weekend totes, cellphone covers, iPod cases), he has been anointed the "Tom Ford of Coach" by his fashion peers.

In Southampton, the Krakoffs' pace of life is almost as swift as it is in the city. "For both Delphine and me, the ideal vacation is some work, some hanging-out time," says Reed. "When people say the Hamptons are too crazy, I say they can always stay home. We would get really bored if we were someplace without a social life."

The two love to exercise their restless spirits by renovating homes for themselves. They have done a total of four together in the past five years, completing the first while they were still

260

dating. (They married in 2003; daughter Lily was born in 2004, and son Oscar in 2005. Reed also has a child from a previous marriage.)

But while their town house on the Upper East Side took more than three years to restore, their house in Southampton took only six months to clean up and furnish, and it looks all the better for it, according to Delphine.

"Doing it faster made it more cohesive," she says. "There was only that one obsession, instead of several competing obsessions."

When the couple first started house shopping, they were in the market for something modern but classic, with enough outside space to indulge a burgeoning interest in large-scale sculpture. It took a long time to find the house, an elegantly proportioned white box in good condition, with a very long driveway and a lawn large enough, at four acres, to buffer it from all the old-school shingled manses of Southampton.

The place was built in the mid-1970s by the late Augusta Maynard, who was a fashionable presence about town and an active member of the Southampton Garden Club. Delphine says she likes to conjure Maynard's chic spirit when she gets up at dawn to do a little design work out on the terrace. With her impish but knowing grin, Delphine possesses the European knack for going casual with high style, combining exquisite jewelry with simple jeans, even before breakfast.

As the Krakoffs restored their new find to pristine condition, their working premise was to make it feel as if outdoors and indoors were one. "It's exactly what I wanted and worth the long search," says Reed of his dwelling. "Modern houses with mature landscapes are rare around here."

The interiors sport the same mix of antique French furniture, seventies finds and contemporary avant-garde pieces that the Krakoffs favor in their Manhattan town house. In the city, however, there are also serious historic pieces by the likes of Jean-Michel Frank and Émile-Jacques Ruhlmann, while in Southampton the emphasis is on new collectibles—history in the making, as it were—for example, a steel coffee table by Garouste & Bonetti and a tree-branch lamp by John Dickinson, the late San Francisco designer.

"In the city the mood is darker, richer, more European," says Reed, lounging in a French forties armchair. Adds Delphine, piping up from a deep white canvas sofa of her own design that was inspired by David Hicks, "Here, we have nothing in a precious wood or that requires real maintenance or might warp or make us worry." As if on cue, daughter Lily cries out from her room down the hall, and Reed lopes off to get her up from a midday nap.

A liberal use of green underscores the indoor-outdoor theme. In the living room there is moss-colored silk-bouclé fabric on a Louis XVI settee, and the David Hicks carpet sports a pattern in white and lime green. Mirrors catch the reflected glow of eternal summer. But this chic informality is anything but careless. Even the

or the waterfall of supple metal rods in a Harry Bertoia sculpture by the window.

As for how these two strong-minded aesthetes make decorating decisions, Delphine says that they agree on just about everything of importance, "but when we don't, it's really bitter." Nonplussed, Reed admits that if he really wants something on which they can't agree, he buys it anyway and keeps it in his office.

"He's good at how it all feels and at putting unexpected things together," says Delphine indulgently. "I'm the boring, rational one who says it's not all going to fit."

Despite their differences, the couple shop together with the shared passion typical of dedicated connoisseurs. They travel, mainly to Paris, but also to London and Los Angeles, to visit dealers and auction houses.

"Some people gamble; others buy cars or couture. This is what's fun for us," he says offhandedly. "It's what feeds our work." The couple's current interests range from designers of the seventies, such as Dickinson and Maria Pergay, to contemporary furniture artists.

And then there is the large-scale sculpture. The couple is now looking for just the right Noguchi. "But I don't want the lawn to look like a sculpture park," Reed says. Luckily for the Krakoffs, more space is on the way. They have commissioned Richard Meier to design a house for them in Palm Beach, which should provide room to indulge in captivating new interests.

living-room decor's most winsome touch, two life-size sculptures of woolly sheep that Lily likes to climb on, have a pedigree; they were made in the late sixties by François-Xavier Lalanne for Yves Saint Laurent.

While the first floor flows freely from Lily's room to living room to kitchen to family media room, the second-floor master-bedroom suite is more of a private lair, complete with fur throws and a fireplace. The palette here is quieter. Reed describes it as an expression of colorlessness, using mostly silvers and blues, as in the rock-crystal andirons Delphine designed for the house

264

FUN HOUSE

Can a house have too much personality? It's a question that doesn't really come up these days—maybe because we'd all secretly rather live with someone else's personality (hello, reality TV home makeover) or with no personality at all (i.e., in a luxury-hotel suite).What we want most from decor right now, it seems, is an escape from ourselves.

Not Manfredi and Dora della Gherardesca. The town house they share with their two children, Aliotto, four, and Margherita, two, on the northern fringes of London's Notting Hill, is a jubilant self-portrait, a realization of the old French proverb *tel le logis, tel le maitre*—essentially, "tell me how your house looks and I'll tell you who you are."

Manfredi, an Italian-born art consultant who runs MDG Fine Arts Ltd., in London, doesn't think there's any other way to live. "I wish that people would express themselves with a little more freedom," he says, weary of preaching his decorating doctrine to the unconverted. "Because in this day and age, you really must create your own aesthetic universe. Every trend has been exploited; every revival has been revived." A quick study in design, Manfredi remembers every setting he has ever admired, from the aristocratic apartment in Florence in which he grew up to a friend's Regency

OVERLEAF: "We are no minimalists," admits Manfredi della Gherardesca of the London house he shares with his wife, Dora, and their two children. Bill Amberg designed the zebra-print pouf.

LEFT: Aliotto, Margherita and Dora carouse.

RIGHT: Manfredi's custom-fitted dressing room, with shoes for each day of the work week.

country house whose doors he cribbed for the town house to the early-eighties New York triplex of Gianni and Marella Agnelli. Gianni's dressing room, with its majestic shirt drawers that disappeared into the wall on smooth-as-silk runners, became the model for Manfredi's "mediocre and very modest imitation."

If Manfredi is the family mockingbird, then Dora, a public-relations consultant and editor, is its magpie. She has a penchant for anything bright, patterned or amusing, which can add up to an awful lot over time. Before the two married in 1998, Dora (officially Princess Maria-Theodora Loewenstein, the London-born daughter of Rolling Stones' business manager Prince Rupert Loewenstein) was living in a cozy Notting Hill apartment packed with clothes, tote bags full of

shoes, designer luggage and Andy Warhol's Mick Jagger silk screens (a gift from the subject), not to mention a kick-pleated sofa and chairs. Moving with Manfredi into a house of several stories sounded like a great idea. The reality became less appealing about eight months after they'd bought a place, however, when their plan for a minor renovation failed to get the required permits. Having fallen in love with the street, they eyed a building under renovation down the block.

"The owner was just about to put in some sort of red glass Philippe Starck things in the bathrooms—very suspicious," Manfredi says with a shudder. "So we told him, 'Stop right there.' We gave him a big fat check and swapped houses. He took our house with the problems, and the fat check, and we took his house, which had no problems and was very advanced in construction." The timing couldn't have been better, since Dora had given birth to Aliotto the week before.

Almost simultaneously they became the proud parents of a baby boy and a double-fronted Edwardian pile of 5,500 square feet spread out over four floors and overlooking a walled garden. The first floor holds the sitting and dining rooms, with a kitchen across the back; the second includes a master suite with twin baths and dressing rooms and the library; the top floor is for the children and guests. Laundry and service quarters are in the basement.

"I was immediately mesmerized by the proportions," says Manfredi, who has been known to help his clients with more than just art advice. ("A lot of people say that I should turn decorating into my profession—it's an idea I toy with. What I need is a client who is quite gutsy.") He set craftsmen to work correcting the alignment of doorways and installing new cornices to replace the decrepit ones barely hanging in place. Within six months, the decoration was complete and the family had started entertaining.

"I was a little put off at first by the formality of a big house and by having staff," admits Dora, an apartment dweller since the age of twenty-two. "But I've gotten used to it, and in retrospect I think I was in the midst of adjusting to the baby's arrival, too." There was also the book she had on the drawing board, a forty-year retrospective of her favorite band. With a new baby to look after and work on the house to supervise while Manfredi scouted art fairs overseas, Dora coped by working part-time from

"Our house is a happy house in part because it doesn't have white walls," says Manfredi, who is fond of the vintage Rose Cumming wallpaper in the master bedroom.

home, converting her new dressing room into an office: "I suddenly realized that I work more effectively when I'm here."

At that point, wouldn't it have been helpful to hand over the decorating to a professional? "Absolutely not," Dora insists. "I really enjoyed doing it myself, as did Manfredi."

It's a good thing, then, that the couple shares a level of visual precociousness you'd more often expect to find in their children. (Margherita was born in 2002.) The sitting room, for instance, has walls of Barbie-friendly lilac, a color Dora suggested and Manfredi seconded, having used it himself in his Earl's Court bachelor flat. She found a matching print fabric to re-cover the four Venetian Rococo chairs Manfredi had inherited, and he chose the room's major accessories: contemporary art, including Dora's suite of Warhol prints; 20th-century ceramics; and his collection of antique narwhal tusks. ("I'm something of a connoisseur at this point," he jokes.) Together they commissioned artist and close friend Oriel Harwood to design a mantel and curtain pelmets faced in mirror shards—a fairy-tale illustration come to life in a room any Surrealist would applaud.

The rest of the house is bursting with additional Rorschachian details. There is Manfredi's preoccupation with culinary ritual, hinted at in the dining room, where groupings of antique Belgian coffeepots and anachronistic serving utensils upstage walls lined with Milanese plates from the 1770s. There is Dora's fixation on comfort, hard to miss in the modern-day opium den that is the library, with its low Moroccan tables, 19th-century French chinoiserie daybed and plump velvet armchairs. Then there is the pair's mutual appreciation of kitsch, running from the velvety pink Buddha coin bank in the entry hall past the Warhol volcano print in the sitting room right through to the strawberry-patterned tiles and glass-fruit chandelier in the kitchen. Dizzying in its references, the Gherardesca *wunderkammer* is nonetheless unique.

"I have this rather Renaissance idea of collecting," Manfredi explains. "I think that things should be able to live together with a certain rhyme and reason. The objects we love the most are the ones that represent stages of our lives. One might say that not everything here goes together or is of top quality, but in my philosophy that's not important. I think an obsessiveness about quality can be a bit stifling—it's not heartwarming, and it also doesn't tell you very much about the owner's intellectual trip."

Whatever trip the Gherardescas plan on taking next isn't certain, but it's bound to generate its own visual corollary. After all, there's a weekend cottage in Badminton to work on. And a house can never have too much personality.

CONSUMMATE GRACE

S AILING ACROSS LAKE WASHINGTON FROM downtown Seattle, you hardly notice the ground-hugging lakefront house that Jim Olson has designed for Barney Ebsworth, even though it extends 230 feet among the trees. Ebsworth wanted an unobtrusive home for his acclaimed collection of American art, so architect Olson, a Northwesterner attuned to the pale, misty light of the region, used concrete, steel, Portuguese limestone and reclaimed red cedar stained the soft color of weathered pine needles. Anyone would covet the forested site, which looks out over still water to the Olympic Mountains, but few would have had the taste and restraint to create such a masterpiece of understatement.

"The house was a project to keep me from getting old," says Ebsworth, who still works out every other day. Like Jay Gatsby, he has come a long way to this lawn beside the water. He grew up in St. Louis, failed in his dream to run in the Olympics but found a new passion during his military service in France. "Every minute I could take, I spent at the Louvre," he recalls, "and that led me to all the other great European art museums." Returning to St. Louis, he got into the travel business and eventually started two cruise lines, Royal and Clipper. He made his initial art acquisitions—four 18th-century Japanese scrolls and a half-dozen 17th-century Dutch paintings—before deciding to focus on modern American art from

OVERLEAF: David Hockney's *Henry Geldzahler and Christopher Scott* (1968–69) fills a living-room wall.

LEFT: Arshile Gorky's *Good Afternoon, Mrs. Lincoln* (1944) hangs above a nickel-plated steel fireplace.

RIGHT: A spiral staircase with panels of bronze plated steel leads up to the master suite.

the first half of the 20th century. In 2000 the resulting collection went on view at the National Gallery of Art, in Washington, D.C., where Ebsworth was cochair of the Collectors Committee.

By the time he sold his travel companies, in 1999, Ebsworth felt ready for a change of scene. His daughter, Christiane, had moved to Chicago, where she is now raising a family; he realized he could relocate to the Northwest, an area he enjoyed, and still be surrounded by good friends, including some of the art lovers and professionals he'd gotten to know while he was building his collection. And so in 2000 Ebsworth found the spectacular lakeside site, tore down an old summer cottage on the property and commissioned a new house, sketching a linear plan that gave every major room a view of the lake, to the west.

"Most clients come with ideas for their houses and we welcome that," says Jim Olson, who's been practicing in his native Seattle for almost forty years. "We took Barney's diagram, developed five or six concepts around it, and he picked the simplest one."

Like his three partners at Olson Sundberg Kundig Allen, the architect is a graduate of the University of Washington; he divides his time between an art-filled city apartment and a family house on Puget Sound. Whereas Ebsworth, with his mane of white hair, cuts a sharp profile in a polo shirt, pants, psychedelic striped socks and Gucci loafers, Olson is as engaging and fuzzy as an Edward Koren cartoon character. His taste runs to heathery tweeds and corduroys, and he has a dreamy air that belies the precision of his work. He's created a score of houses locally and farther afield that are rooted in their landscapes and that guide their occupants through a progression of finely proportioned spaces. Art collectors seek him out for his mastery of volume and light, and for the refinement of his details. It's no surprise that two of the architectural legends he most admires are Louis Kahn, author of the luminous Kimbell Art Museum, in Fort Worth, and the Venetian Carlo Scarpa, who subtly modulated palaces and castles in the Veneto region to suit their new roles as art museums.

LEFT: When he found the lakefront site, Barney Ebsworth (with his Old English sheepdogs) was drawn to its monumental western red cedars and Douglas firs.

RIGHT: Olson worked the house in around the trees, cutting down only two in the building process. The sloping lawn is landscaped with rhododendrons and other shrubs.

At the Ebsworth house, Olson achieved an easy balance of architecture, art and nature, drawing on the aesthetic traditions of Japan. Shallow-pitched eaves seem to hover over the long, low facade and the succession of rooms that flow one into the next from north to south along the lake. Trees conceal much of the approach from the east, parting to reveal a central hall that runs from the steel-and-wood entry canopy through the center of the house to a wall of glass that frames a view of the lake and silhouettes a massive bronze nude by Gaston Lachaise. Cutting across this hall is an extended lakeside gallery leading to the master suite at the north end and guest accommodations to the south. There the ground naturally drops away, and a glass bridge links the gallery to the guest sitting room,

embowered in the treetops. Stairs lead down to two bedrooms, tucked in below.

"I wanted the house to melt into the forest," says Olson, "and the interiors to feel as though they were floating in light." Working with Seattle interior designer Terry Hunziker on colors and finishes, he has realized both goals.

Ebsworth treats his residence as a campus of distinct living areas, retiring to his office or the den in the master suite when he's alone but sharing every part of the house with frequent visitors. "Barney loves to entertain, and the house has a civic as well as a private character," Olson observes. One of its more intimate aspects is a glass-enclosed master shower that juts into a walled Japanese garden, allowing the owner to bathe amid scarlet maples in the fall. A small elevator rises to a belvedere overlooking the various rooflines and canopies that evoke one of Wright's Midwestern prairie houses.

Ebsworth also enjoys hosting the occasional museum benefit, and recounting how he became to own his many treasures.

"I realized I'd never acquire the best works or the expertise in the Old Masters field, so I consulted Charles Buckley, then the director of the Saint Louis Art Museum," Ebsworth says. Buckley encouraged him to collect early American modernists, and from there he moved on to later American painters.

In the living room, David Hockney's double portrait *Henry Geldzahler and Christopher Scott* (1968–69) and Jasper Johns's *Gray Rectangles* (1957) dominate the walls. Those two major post-1955 works and William Glackens's 1914 Impressionist study of a girl in a café bracket a collection that is centered on Georgia O'Keeffe, Charles Sheeler, Alexander Calder and contemporaries who will one day be much better known. Having commissioned a house for his art, Ebsworth is now turning to Tadao Ando, the Japanese architect, to design a public chapel in the Seattle area that Ebsworth is dedicating to his parents. Though the site has not yet been finalized, the place of worship is likely to inspire future generations of Northwestern architects to flights of creativity.

MAINE
MAN

ALEX KATZ STANDS, ON A BRILLIANT summer day, in front of the yellow foursquare house instantly recognizable from many of his paintings. "This is it," the artist says, forty-odd years of profound affection summed up in the economical statement. He gestures with a squash player's sinewy arms toward the Maine woods, marshes, fields and sky around him. "I like being here," his succinct explanation goes, "because everywhere you look is, what do you call it . . . beautiful."

Alex Katz and Maine have been friends for a long time. One of the busier social figures on New York's winter art scene, the painter decamps every June for the Northeast, and solitude. Far from any kindred community or artists' colony (the Skowhegan School of Painting and Sculpture that first introduced him to the region in 1949 is seventy-five miles away), Katz and his wife, Ada, his perpetual subject and muse, embrace a quiet existence surprising for an artist commonly identified with stylized depictions of sophisticated couples choreographed in sleekly urbane tableaux. In recent years, particularly, wonderful large-scale landscapes have welled up out of Katz's ever-deeper attachment to the Maine countryside, winning him new critical respect—in fact, some of the best reviews of his career.

Katz has had to wait for this moment. As an artist, he has

Katz stenciled the entryway walls of his cottage in an egg-and-cross pattern made with a potato stamp.

made his own way, pioneering what he himself dubbed "post-abstractionism": the reconciliation of realism with modernist abstraction and its aftermath. Raised in Queens, New York, the son of a Russian Jewish coffee merchant and an actress on the Yiddish stage, he initially planned to take the safe path of commercial art. But following his graduation from Cooper Union in Manhattan, he was increasingly lured by the avant-garde studio work of the New York School painters then headed for their heyday. He became friendly with the group, but set out in a different direction stylistically. He has never looked back.

The reinvigoration of Katz's landscape work has coincided with his longer and longer sojourns at the 19th-century farmhouse he owns in Lincolnville, the tiny town near Penobscot

Bay that Katz says has barely changed since he bought his place in the early fifties. Maine seems made for him. Its puritanical reticence matches his flinty reserve; its Waspy informality suits his elegant nonchalance. And though he may not voice it, Katz also enjoys carrying on an American tradition, rooted in the 19th century, in which artists have recorded their intense passion for this stringent, dramatic, vigorous region of natural beauty and human struggle.

He has worked on his land here as hard as any Yankee farmer, pruning and planting and stripping and mowing to achieve his ideal landscape, its straight lines, flat surfaces and uncluttered ambiance all finding their way into his art. For seven years the unassuming cottage on the property had no electricity, and Katz liked it that way. "At one point I thought of selling this place and buying something bigger and grander," he says. But he didn't. Instead, the diminutive house has kept him close to the outdoor world he has called on continually in the process of developing his signature style.

Inside, the house itself has come to resemble a Katz painting in three dimensions. Colors are strong and startling; furnishings possess the bold outlines of Katz's trademark figures. When he was young and poor, he decorated the entrance hall with a handsome repeat egg-and-cross pattern, made with a potato stamp; now successful and wealthy, he has kept this resourceful handi-work, along with the resolutely unpretentious furniture he acquired back in those days. The simple geometry of antique cabinets and eccentric secondhand folk pieces is highlighted against walls of Matissean pink in the music room, robin's-egg blue in the bedroom, sunflower yellow and sienna elsewhere. Throughout the house, Katz's portraits are juxtaposed with found objects recycled from the woods and the shore.

"I like to tinker," says Katz, and so, it turns out, does Ada. One of the artist's restoration projects, a Victorian square grand piano, now sits in the music room at the front of the house. In the step-up kitchen nearby, cooking is done on a Detroit Jewel range from the thirties, purchased (for $7) more for its good looks than for any promise that it might work; but Ada figured out the inner mechanics, and now it produces savory pasta dinners for the Katzes and their occasional guests, most frequently their son Vincent and his wife, Vivien. Beyond the kitchen is the dining room, formerly Katz's studio and originally an attached horse barn.

In 1987 the artist built a new studio overlooking a nearby marsh. Its shingled, angular composition, the work of Japanese American architect Frank Kawasaki, is loosely modeled on Japanese temple architecture; the soaring interior walls are positioned to capture just the right light for the small, painstaking studies Katz makes there in preparation for each huge finished work he will create back in Manhattan come fall.

Katz cruises his Yankee paradise in a 1975 baby-blue Cadillac convertible, absorbing the indigenous sights that will enter his art. "There are lots of good ice-cream signs," he notices.

The artist's attraction to the American vernacular extends not just to ice-cream signs, Colonial portraiture, folk art and billboards but also to those homegrown fifties artifacts, the snapshot and the home movie. Abstracted and enlarged on his enormous canvases, these elements inform his off-kilter cropping and successful capturing of the subtleties of every season and time of day. Katz has a ceaseless fascination with light. "Light is the most interesting thing we have," he says. "American light, the type I use, is a quick light. It's more instantaneous than the slow light of European art. My style is completely American."

Light is the glory of the place that holds him as an artist. American painters from Winslow Homer and Rockwell Kent to Jamie Wyeth and Neil Welliver have fallen for Maine because its light endowed their art with a liberating new lease on landscape painting. In Katz's case, it illuminates the particulars he responds to in his summertime locale: a house, a workplace, a regimented tranquillity that have contributed to his unmistakable style and body of work.

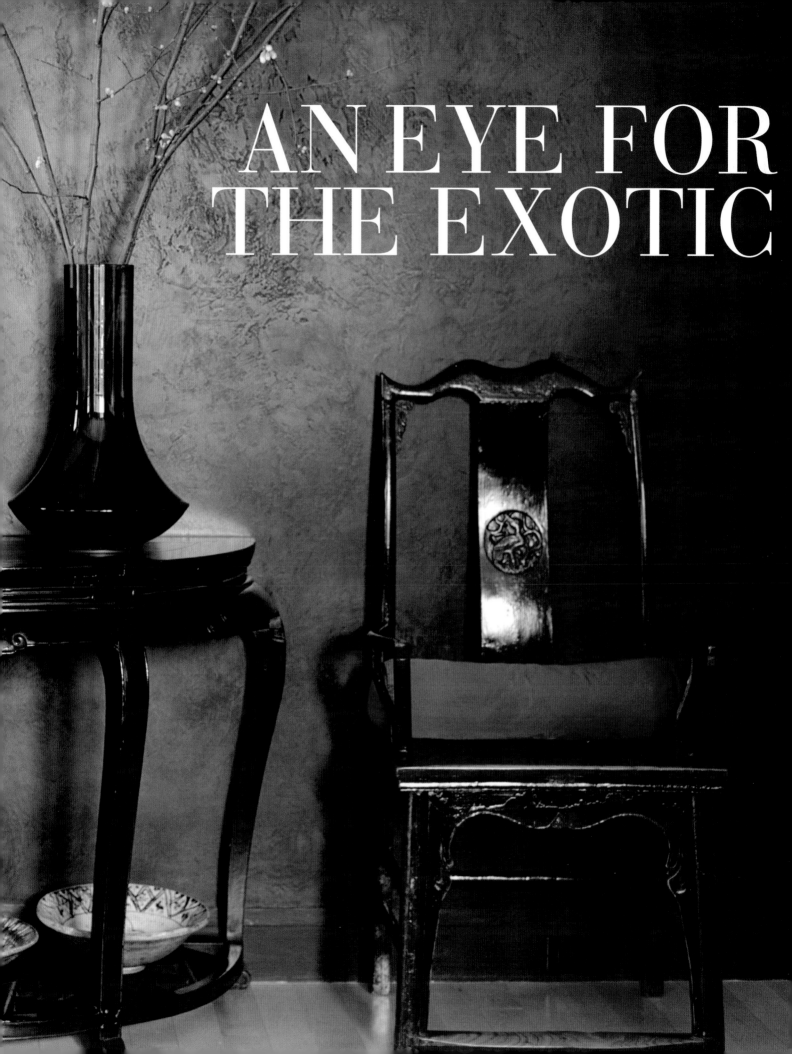

AN EYE FOR
THE EXOTIC

OVERLEAF: A waxed-plaster wall divides Sherri Donghia's kitchen and living area. Also in the mix: Chinese furniture, Murano glass vases and Islamic ceramics.

RIGHT: A Chinese altar table holding Turkish and Thai head-pieces and a German anglepoise lamp rests beneath framed textiles from India and Persia.

I'M AN IDIOSYNCRATIC COLLECTOR," ADMITS NEW Yorker Sherri Donghia.

Actually, "idiosyncratic" is far too small a word to encompass the wildly varied treasures that Sherri, an independent textile designer and home furnishings consultant, displays in her loft in Manhattan's TriBeCa. For here, even to enter the front door, one must first use both arms to part the thick folds of colorfully striped fabric from a Bedouin tent that hangs just inside.

"It's from one of the 'stans," she says, running her fingers over the patched and sun-bleached cloth. She is referring specifically to Turkmenistan, Afghanistan and Pakistan—all far-flung places she's studied enough to dub by their shared last syllable.

Once inside, Sherri, who sometimes refers to herself as a 21st-century nomad, describes the provenance of other souvenirs close at hand, ranging from Mexican mercury-glass balls and Turkish headpieces to Chinese scholar chairs and amber bracelets from Russia. She also owns a world tour's trove of textiles. She cheerfully expounds on each example, be it contemporary Vietnamese patchwork or a rare fragment from the Ottoman Empire embroidered with metal thread in a technique called zari.

OVERLEAF: A bowl full of worldly jewelry; an embroidered paisley spread covers the bed, whose headboard is upholstered with antique Indian sari fabric.

LEFT: New Venetian glass, including a lamp and a vase from Donghia, tops an antique Italian table.

RIGHT: An English silver tea set sits on an Indian cloth embroidered with silver threads.

Such lessons often emerge spontaneously, given the casual way Sherri has chosen to display her possessions in this spot where she's lived with her husband, Roger Eulau, a commercial-real-estate broker, for the past seven years. Objects and furnishings frequently change places, she says, and on a whim may be rotated among the loft, her office a few blocks away and the couple's weekend house in East Hampton.

And while at first it's hard to find a through line in this mesmerizing mélange, Sherri, whose speech is interwoven with the terminology of cloth making, believes there is a "common thread."

"Everything I collect has patina, character and depth because you can see the human hand," she explains. "I also believe things that are frayed and faded bring positive energy to a space."

In a former, longtime role as design director for the Donghia home furnishings company, she carried on the legacy of her late cousin, the interiors and furniture designer Angelo Donghia, who founded the business in 1969. Once she assumed the creative helm, a position she held for seventeen years, Sherri built a reputation as a textile designer of international renown. Her inspiration continues to spring from how deeply she cares about subtleties in the aesthetic process. The attention she pays to such nuances is almost her form of spirituality.

Indeed, Sherri has been reading up lately on wabi-sabi, a Japanese aesthetic principle with roots in Zen Buddhism, which celebrates impermanence and irregularity in the natural world. "The basic idea of wabi-sabi is that imperfection is what gives an object a soul," she says.

Sherri, who grew up in Vandergrift, a small town in western Pennsylvania, says that local thrift stores were her first window to a wider world. To this day, she still frequents the Ladies Village Improvement Society resale shop in East Hampton.

It was, however, her work as a young assistant at Bloomingdale's—where she was mentored by Katie Murphy, the store's famed fashion director in the early 1970s—that allowed her curiosity to take flight and span the globe. Recalling these early travels, Sherri points out that she wasn't a tourist but was working to develop new products and

ferret out design sources abroad. Hence, her first look at places like India or Indonesia was guided by the aesthetic sensibilities of artisans. Her wanderlust widened during her subsequent stints as a developer of new products for Federated Department Stores and the retail shops at RockResorts, which was founded by the late Laurance Rockefeller.

"When you are enthusiastic about learning about someone's craft, it nearly becomes another language, and people are happy to talk with you," she says. And while many business travelers tether themselves to home while on the road—constantly fiddling with PDAs and international cell phones—Sherri tries to blend in as quickly as possible, sometimes even donning local mufti, such as hand-tooled tunics in Muslim countries.

"I want my eyes to be opened to unusual things," she says. By making scrapbooks of her trips that combine handwritten notes, pieces of cloth, sketches and photographs, she creates a two-way street. Her collecting influences her designs; designing informs what she collects.

"Sherri is always hungry for new experiences. She's voracious, really," remarks Stephanie Odegard, a friend and fellow designer who frequently collaborates with her on floor coverings. "Sometimes I talk to her husband when she's off traveling, and only once in all these years has he reported that she was unhappy. As Roger says, 'If Sherri can't find something to be excited about, the place must be pretty dreary.'"

And drearier if she can't find something to buy. For she nearly always spots an object she has to have, be it jewelry, silver, coral or a remnant of cloth. She thinks nothing of dragging home unwieldy bundles, such as the canvas bag she carried onto a plane that held a disassembled antique Murano crystal chandelier, now hanging in her home office, that she'd found at a London flea market.

Asked which one fabric she loves above all, Sherri answers without hesitation, "Linen. I love that it marks and wrinkles." She then strokes the brown linen-velvet fabric by Donghia that's covering a chair. When her touch creates shimmering variations of color, she laughs with delight. "See? Instant patina!"

MAKING A HOME FOR ART

Some people think of art as all the decor they need; give them a few roomfuls of choice paintings, and they'll be happy living in an empty apartment. Others think of furnishings as art enough; give them a sofa and chairs by someone named George—Hepplewhite, Nelson, Nakashima—or Marc—du Plantier, Newson—and they're all set. Between these two poles lie the rest of us, and many of the subjects in this book. Appreciative of art, design, decorative arts and architecture, we look for the most poetic ways of bringing our loves together.

Obviously, the approaches that can be taken to living with art and design at home are almost as numerous as the kinds of objects you might choose to live with. And yet it's useful to compare your own ideas with those of others in similar situations, especially when you're in the process of building a collection, moving house or rethinking an interior.

ADAPTIVE REUSE: THE DE LA CRUZES

The true collector is someone who suddenly realizes that they've bought more than they can display, but they can't bear to think of moving. Is that you? The scenario certainly describes Rosa and Carlos de la Cruz of Miami. When they started collecting contemporary art in the late 1980s, the de la Cruzes hung it in rooms filled with French furniture and oriental carpets in their Key Biscayne home. A decade later, they painted their interior white, replaced the French furniture with 20th-century classics, including a set of Frank Gehry's bentwood chairs, and built a 5,000-square-foot addition to their modernist house, opening it to the public on a limited basis. Despite the addition, they have so much art that it crowds into the kitchen and even the laundry room—both of which become part of the public tour each December when the couple host their annual open house for Art Basel Miami Beach. (An upstairs bedroom wing remains off-limits.) Recently the de la Cruzes decided to open a building in the Miami design district dedicated

Blue chip art, both fine and decorative, communes in the Paris living room of Giancarlo Giammetti, designed by Peter Marino.

ABOVE: *Rosa de la Cruz at home in Key Biscayne with work by Marco Boggio-Sella.*

RIGHT: *Architect and designer Stephen Miller Siegel chose African matting to accompany a Chinese screen in this New York City apartment.*

to displaying their collection—what can't fit into the house, that is. It will be interesting to see whether the house, in giving up its role as part-time gallery, reclaims some of the intimacy it lost in being "white-cubed."

NATURAL PAIRINGS: ROBERT ROSENKRANZ

Another successful pairing is that of French Art Deco furniture and Chinese art. Eastern arts and crafts inspired the makers of French furniture in the Deco period, and the natural affinity between the two is obvious in the Manhattan apartment of Robert Rosenkranz, designed by New Yorkers Carey Maloney and Hermes Mallea of (M) Group. The collector began with Wiener Werkstätte furniture, then moved on to French pieces from the Art Deco period; he came later to Chinese art. Now the collections meet in Rosenkranz's apartment overlooking the East River in Manhattan. Indeed, the pairing is so smooth that both elements risk receding slightly into a unified decorative "scheme"— until you look more closely at the high level of the work itself. The Tang dynasty horse in the living room may be the best in New York; the majestic pen-and-ink drawing by Liu Dan in the entry hall is a tour-de-force. Edgar Brandt, Émile-Jacques Ruhlmann and Robert Mallet-Stevens are all represented in the furniture collection.

MIX, OR MATCH?

One of the intriguing things about time-tested combinations of art and interiors is that the combination strategies themselves reflect a sense of history. In the 1950s, modernist residential architecture dictated an entirely new way of living, and that meant new interiors—new in the 1950s, that is. Today many 1950s houses still proudly display furniture concurrent with the architecture—and the two seem made for each other to a degree few pairings do. New York furniture dealer Barry Friedman and his family own a 1953 Marcel Breuer house north of the city; he takes great pleasure in furnishing it with treasures of midcentury fine and

European modern furnishings complement a collection of black and white photography in this Manhattan dining room, designed by Stephen Miller Siegel.

decorative arts, including furniture, glass, lighting and even a vintage (and nonfunctioning) stereo.

Today such matched relationships are out of fashion, though they continue to be as potent and insightful as ever. On the flip side, people are discovering that profoundly beautiful juxtapositions of art and furniture can result from what you might call adverse conditions: a low-ceilinged room that makes a large painting seem more intimate, or a steel and glass house that draws attention to the humanity of early American furniture. But successful interior relationships are usually easier to pull off when you choose a setting (or have it custom-built) for a collection, or a collection is amassed for a specific setting. In this chapter, Olson Sundberg Kundig Allen's lakeside house for Barney Ebsworth honors a top collection of 20th-century American painting without losing its sensitivity to the setting or the client's needs. Architect Tadao Ando's Invisible House, on the other hand, was designed without specific holdings in mind. But the masterwork in the Italian Veneto has inspired its owner, Alessandro Benetton, to acquire art that suits its rough glamour, including paintings by Lucio Fontana and Jean-Michel Basquiat.

MAKING A NEW SPACE FOR ART

One of the chief benefits to building a house from scratch, or adding dedicated gallery space, is that an architect can tailor the space to suit the special needs of your collection, whether it's video art, complex installation work, light-sensitive drawings or textiles or classical statuary. For a young and acquisitive collector of contemporary painting and sculpture in Los Angeles, the Santa Monica–based architecture firm of Marmol Radziner went so far as to line the interior walls of a 1950s house on a hillside with half-inch plywood panels behind the sheetrock, so that work could be hung securely in any location and could also be moved around freely without risk.

WHY BUILD A SPACE FOR ART AFRESH?

■ A mature collection can be treated more like a museum installation, and a hanging scheme worked out at the time the architectural plans are coming together.

■ Wall dimensions and lighting conditions can be factored into the design, which can provide the ideal viewing conditions for a particular piece, on the understanding that it probably won't be moving. Jim Olson, of Olson Sundberg Kundig Allen, often suggests giving an important work a wall of its own, rather than making it one in a line of pieces hanging, gallery-style, at eye level.

■ Another benefit to building your own square footage for art is that you can address the many practicalities that come with collecting head-on, instead of trying to retrofit a space. For example, it's useful to have a roomy and secure place for unloading and unpacking objects and moving them into the house.

■ You'll also want a proper security system, temperature and humidity management systems and a lighting system to prevent damage (and to keep your insurance premiums under control). And consider including a dedicated office for managing the collection, where you can store records, computer equipment and related literature.

■ The bulk of your art storage can be handled off-site, but if you collect photography, works on paper, books or small canvases, you'll want some fireproof storage for small works at home. With a dedicated art facility, you can do that.

LIGHTING MATTERS

Whether you build for your holdings or not, the one aspect you shouldn't overlook is lighting. Not only does proper lighting add to an appreciation of what you have, it can conserve what you have, ensuring that others after you can enjoy it. Ideally you'll consider hiring a lighting consultant when you rearrange a collection or plan a new space. If your

Wayne Thiebaud's Bakery Counter *(1962) gets a wall of its own in Barney Ebsworth's Seattle dining room, designed by Jim Olson.*

ABOVE: *Mix, not match, say Blair and Alistair Clarke, whose Manhattan dining room features new art amid 18th-century decor.*

RIGHT: *Sculptural 20th-century furniture is a quiet foil for Peter Coffin's whirling* Rainbow *(2005) in Catherine Rose's Dallas living room.*

designer or architect doesn't already work with a reputable consultant, contact the International Association of Lighting Designers (visit iald.org for a list of members). A lighting designer will consider the architectural features of the rooms, the orientation of the natural light sources and the nature of the work itself. While drawings and photographs are known to have special lighting needs, the same is also true of textiles and costumes, sculpture and even oil painting; direct sunlight can cause fugitive pigments to change color. Watch out for heat buildup and ultraviolet light exposure as well as direct sun. These can cause surfaces to yellow, crack or fade.

Steven Heffernan, a lighting consultant who has advised museums and galleries nationwide, has these specific suggestions for lighting three-dimensional objects.

■ "The play of light and shadow on three dimensions is essential in revealing form, detail and texture," he points out. "This is particularly the case with pieces that are translucent, such as sculptural glass. The placement of the light source is critical—and several lights may be needed."

■ "Textiles and tapestries also require special consideration. A raking light, set at an angle to the surface, could bring out imperfections, while a diffuse light could wash out all the texture."

■ When lighting objects that are behind glass, Heffernan suggests that "moving lights closer to the wall on which the object is hung may remove the reflection. If that isn't possible, place a light to either side—there will be no reflections from the straight-on viewing position."

■ Finally, Heffernan points out that there is no one right way to light anything. "Lighting design is a process of sculpting visual perceptions. And art is in the eye of the beholder. Lighting designers don't dare get between people and their ideas of what constitutes a worthy collection."

CHAPTER FOUR

GLORIOUS GETAWAYS

HOW FAR CAN YOU GET AWAY THESE DAYS? Thanks to the inventiveness of interior design and architecture, pretty far. If you're Dodie Rosekrans of San Francisco, for example, your decor can be even wilder than the shores you've chosen to rest upon—in her case, Hollywood Renaissance style in a palazzo on the Grand Canal of Venice. *Town & Country* lives for a good escape, and we usually find it in the fantasy-fueled houses that people like Rosekrans are inspired to create. By definition, getaways are never full-time dwellings, which grants them the license to be a bit more imaginative than a main residence would be. If a house is planned within an existing resort community, a fanciful design might be encouraged or even prescribed (as at the Palmeraie, in Marrakech). Such Xanadus are fewer and fewer these days, however. The building guidelines enforced in most new resort areas tend to be conservative, historically based and without room for experimentation. Frustrated fans of Chinoiserie and the like can console themselves with this thought: several thousand years ago, what we built reflected just three things—the local climate, the materials available and how many of those materials we could afford. These conditions led to the development of the regional styles we love so much today. A successful modern house, no matter the style, is still informed by the same three basic conditions. Look closely at the houses in this chapter. A beach retreat has porches to catch prevailing winds in any direction; a Mexican getaway is built with cool stone floors. Elsie de Wolfe's famous dictum, "Suitability, suitability, suitability," still has its place, even at the ends of the earth.

Liz and Martin Landau's pool at their Marrakech home.

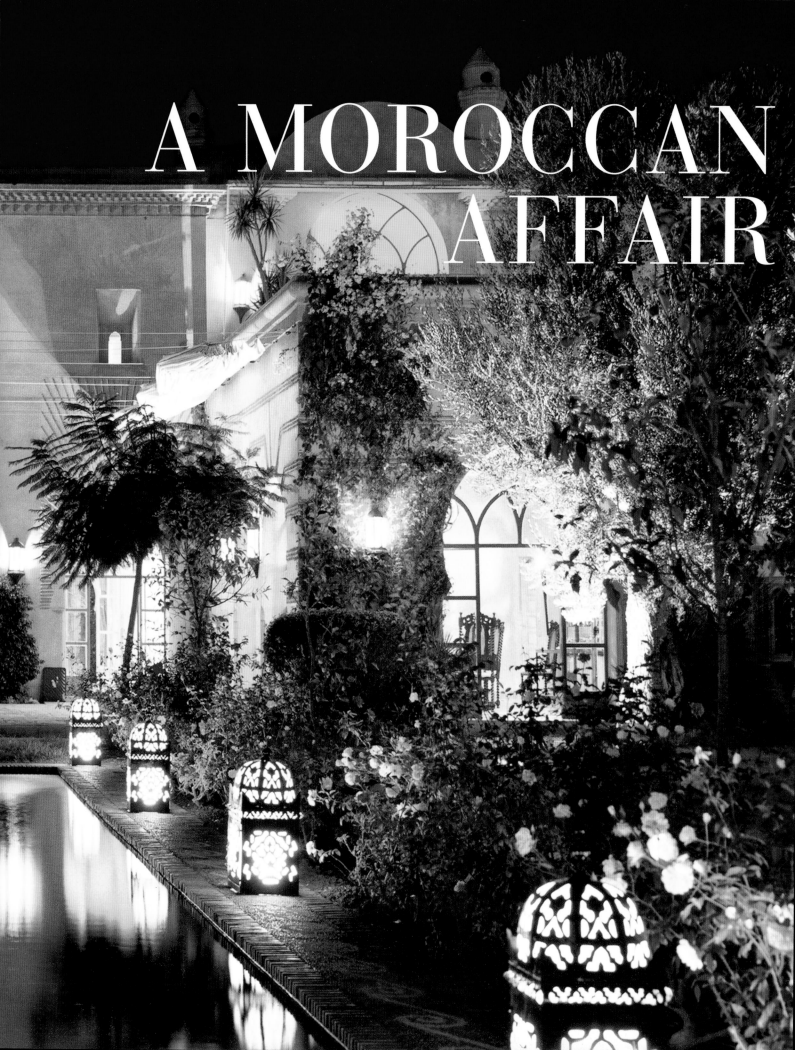

A MOROCCAN
AFFAIR

WE'RE HALFWAY ACROSS MARRAKECH'S main square—the Djemaa el Fna—when the heavens open up. It pours, and even my rain-resistant traveling companions are glad to see the legion of umbrella purveyors who have instantly materialized before us. Sad to say, our driver does not materialize with the same alacrity. Eventually, rather damp, we're on our way, windshield wipers scraping furiously, to the Palmeraie—the historic palm grove twenty minutes north of town where, since the mid-nineties, some of the city's most sumptuous residential estates have blossomed like exotic flowers in a lunar landscape.

Dusk falls with a boom as we bump along the rutted roads toward this optimistically named oasis. Then we pass through the towered gates of Manzah al Jamil. Dramatic lighting plays across glistening lakes and luxuriant gardens as we roll up the winding drive. When the house suddenly appears, on the top of a rise around the last bend, it more than lives up to the picturesque prelude. A majestic Moroccan palace, built by British property investor and developer Martin Landau and his wife, Liz, it is a triumphant blend of oriental style and luxurious Western comfort.

The Landaus' charming majordomo, Saïd Flilis, leads us up terraced stone steps alongside a series of cascading ornamental pools planted with papyrus and lilies and stocked with fish. At

The Landaus' home has numerous secluded spaces, such as this outdoor dining alcove off a terrace. "It's a property where people can do lots of things in different parts of the house and garden," says Martin.

the top, we walk through the entrance loggia to a heavy wooden door carved with camel motifs. We're definitely in Morocco.

Liz's plane has been delayed by the storm, so Saïd shows us around. A vaulted gallery with a polished marble floor runs the length of the two-story house. To the left is the grand salon, with a central portion whose painted ceiling—look up—soars twenty-six feet above. An Aubusson tapestry hangs in the hall; another decorates the large dining room. Four guest bedrooms are as spacious and as well equipped as a master suite; the actual master suite, upstairs, is more of a master wing, with a gym and dressing rooms. Up here, too, is a large winter living room with red-velvet-covered sofas.

When Liz arrives—in pants and leather jacket, and as slim and blonde as in her modeling days—she's fizzing with energy. We plot our program for the next day, which will start with an early visit to the market for flowers and food. Martin will arrive with more guests in the evening.

The next morning the sun reappears, and the full magnificence of this 21,500-square-foot, indoor-outdoor house is revealed. This is not the typical North African architecture of small windows and dark, vividly colored rooms. Instead, light floods through large arched windows into airy spaces painted in neutral shades and earth tones. Interiors blend into exteriors. The eye floats over a tiled terrace and a marble fountain

to a reflecting pool banked with roses and on to a swimming pool in the distance. Greenery is splashed with the blooms of bougainvillea, oleander, jasmine and jacaranda; lawns are studded with olive and orange trees and, of course, towering palms. This is an emerald oasis.

For Liz, whose passionate project it is, the house is also something of a hard-earned miracle. "If you buy an old house and you have to make changes, that is one thing," Martin explains over drinks that evening. "But if you start from scratch and it turns out wrong, you can't blame anybody else but yourselves. Therefore, you better make darn certain that you think it through. That's what we did, and that's why it's worked out really well."

The story of the villa's two-and-a-half-year construction, completed in 2003, has as many twists and turns, setbacks and successes, as any Arabian fairy tale. To understand the plot, one needs to understand the Landau lifestyle. This couple lives between their homes in London, Monte Carlo and Beaulieu. Business takes them farther afield. Martin's company, European Hotels Corporation, invests in such projects as the ultraluxe Four Seasons in Langkawi, Malaysia; the Marrakech Four Seasons, opened in 2008; and the Raffles resorts in Phang Nga, Thailand, and Da Nang, Vietnam.

When they were looking for a new holiday destination, it had to be easily accessible for

OVERLEAF: A loggia overlooking the garden includes a sofa and chairs made for the Landaus in Bali (left); An outdoor alcove is set for tea (right).

LEFT: A wide gallery runs through the house.

RIGHT: The Landaus take a break on the terrace.

"amusing weekends not too far from London." Marrakech was just a three-hour flight away. Liz had loved the country for years; Martin took some convincing. Eventually, after his sixtieth-birthday party (when the Landaus hosted about fifty friends at the La Mamounia hotel) and two subsequent summers renting here, he was up for finding some land to build on.

The couple acquired three plots to make a seven-acre triangle. Getting permission to change the land from agricultural to residential use took six months. For a Westerner, renovating a *riad* in Marrakech's old medina quarter is an exploit; building from scratch is a leap into the unknown. The Landaus designed their house in collaboration with Charles Boccara, a Tunisian-born and Moroccan-educated architect who trained at Paris's École des Beaux-Arts. Known as the king of *tadelakt* (the traditional Moroccan polished-plaster wall treatment that he was instrumental in reviving), Boccara has had a legendary influence on contemporary Marrakech decor through his designs for private houses, hotels and the city's Théâtre Royal.

"Charles had some ideas interpreted into plans and drawings. What we then jointly did with him was to put greater definition into those concepts," Martin says. Getting price and scheduling estimates was an ongoing issue. "We had them, but only by my absolutely nailing people down," Martin says.

Six months into the project, the 9/11 attacks occurred. "Tourism dropped off. La Mamounia was empty; we were sitting by the pool on our own," Liz recalls. But Martin held firm. "I said, 'I'm into the game. Let's have a go.'" They hired local workers, some of whom were housed on the property during construction.

As a veteran of six homes that she has organized for Martin and herself, Liz is an exacting client. One priority from the start was that each bedroom have its own private loggia and a substantial bathroom equipped with shower, tub and well-lighted dressing table. She also insisted on air-conditioning and heating.

Liz's "amalgam of Morocco/modern" is a mix of classic Marrakechi craftsmanship and a light, modern palette. "I wanted the sculpted

321

plaster, painted ceilings, floor tiles and *tadelakt* walls to be in cool cream colors rather than in the traditional multicolored effect," she says. The painted ceiling, its design copied from an old Moroccan palace, took seven months to make and was put up in sections. A very talented metalsmith created the graceful work of the poolside gazebo and the stairway handrail of engraved *maillechort,* an alloy of copper, nickel and zinc, with a silvery sheen that doesn't tarnish.

Aesthetics sometimes clashed with practicalities. "When Charles designed half-moon marble baths and I asked for ordinary large ones that one can stretch out in, he was horrified," Liz says. "He's an artist, and I'm running a comfortable house. It was a huge tussle, but I got everything I wanted in the end."

After the construction phase had finished, the final fine-tuning phase began. "At the start of the project, I came once a month, then every two weeks, and finally, the last six weeks, I stayed in a little hotel nearby and arrived at the house every morning at 8 A.M.," Liz recounts. "Shouts and tears" is how Martin a describes the ordeal. "Every morning there was a new drama, another catastrophe," Liz adds. "Because of a serious leak in the swimming pool, we had to dig a three-meter-deep channel from the pool to the plant room across all the tiles—a complete nightmare."

Now, thanks to a devoted staff of twelve, staying at the house has become a delight. Furnishings feature a meld of early English oak antiques and cushy contemporary sofas and armchairs. Many elements—from a Chinese cabinet, lanterns and lamps to marble fountains and four-poster beds—were made to measure by local artisans. All blend happily with the Orientalist backdrop.

About once a month in spring and fall, Liz comes for a week and Martin arrives with houseguests for long Thursday-to-Tuesday weekends. Martin organizes golf games (he's a member of three courses here; Liz leads shopping expeditions to her own insider finds (a talent she'll put to use by purchasing for the hotel boutique at the Marrakech Four Seasons). They'll do dinner at one of Marrakech's great restaurants or head into the mountains for a desert excursion.

Even after the turmoil of building from scratch, Martin says he would do it all again, although maybe differently. He pays tribute to his wife. "The success of the house is a combination of Liz's wonderful determination and her huge attention to detail," he says.

As for Liz: "It's not like coming home, but like feeling at home, and having an empathy with the people. You see how charming they are." Of all her residences, Manzah al Jamil is closest to her heart. "This is my baby, my folly, my dream," she says, smiling.

VENETIAN FANTASY

DODIE AND JOHN ROSEKRANS, THE SAN Francisco art collectors and philanthropists, would have intrigued Henry James. Since the late 1990s, they've taken first Paris and now Venice by storm; finding themselves in the midst of the art and fashion worlds in both cities, they have become renowned for high-style entertaining in the extraordinary residences they've established. No question that John, in his impeccable Savile Row suits, and the diminutive Dodie, in creations by her favorite designers—Balmain, Gaultier and Galliano—love an adventure. The couple's European odyssey could be taken a lot further, Dodie admits, if only "I felt confident to handle more than four houses. There are many exotic places I'd like to give a try."

Time, not confidence, would have to be the issue here, as the couple seem to create a stir wherever they go. Though John sold his interests in a successful toy company a few years ago, he and Dodie are now involved in supporting medical research and the arts, a tradition that dates back generations in both their families.

In addition to their two homes abroad, they maintain a 1917 Pacific Heights mansion in San Francisco, as well as the 120-acre Runnymede Sculpture Farm in nearby Woodside. (The latest piece on its way to Runnymede: Tom Sachs's controversial *Chanel Guillotine*, an ironic commentary on French history and commerce.)

master of all the decorative arts. Discovered by Elsie de Wolfe in 1941, he designed interiors, jewelry, movie and theater sets and much more, winning a Tony award in 1961 for his costumes for the original Broadway production of *Camelot*. His creative partner, Hutton Wilkinson, who now carries on the Duquette design and jewelry businesses, was an indispensable cohort who took on an increasingly large role in the project as it progressed.

Though the Rosekranses originally intended to find a second European home in France, it wasn't long before Venice came to mind. "It has a very informal feeling, yet it is immersed in a fabulous old culture, which I adore," Dodie explains. "It's wonderful in the summertime. But I love the winters, when it has at times a fog that is so beautiful, romantic and mysterious. And a lot of the best things about Venice are free: the architecture, the life in the piazzas, and the constant pageantry of the Grand Canal."

After a month of house-hunting from the Hotel Cipriani, the couple decided to rent an apartment while they continued their search. It was then that friends suggested looking at the Palazzo Brandolini, a centuries-old building that occupies one of the most majestic sites on the Grand Canal. Count and Countess Brandolini d'Adda reside in an apartment there, as does their son Brandino and his family. But the pièce

"John has always bought pieces he loves," explains Dodie. "He's never asked for advice. He's just bought what he likes. We've ended up with some wonderful things."

Both husband and wife share a flair for seeking out uncommon beauty. Their pied-à-terre in Paris's seventh arrondissement is an Orientalist escape by Los Angeles interior designers Tony Duquette and Hutton Wilkinson that quickly became the talk of the town. Eighteen months after its completion, Dodie called on the same design team to produce a "Venetian fantasy" in one of the most spectacular palazzos along the Grand Canal, with views to rival a Canaletto painting.

It was a sage choice. Tony Duquette, who passed away in 1999, at eighty-five, just months after completing the Venetian project, was a

de résistance is the *piano nobile*—the second, "noble," floor of the palazzo—where the elaborate public reception rooms are located. The Brandolini family had not used the sumptuous rooms for many years, and they were willing to rent out the entire floor.

When the Brandolinis offered a long-term lease on the apartment, there was just one stipulation: that the walls of many of the salons, which had been decorated by the late Renzo Mongiardino in the 1960s, not be permanently altered.

That constraint did little to thwart the designers. Duquette, even in his eighties, never lost the art of play—exactly what was called for to invigorate the magnificent rooms. "When Dodie hired us, she said she wanted a Venetian fantasy—not a literal re-creation," Wilkinson recalls. "That's unusual in Venice. If it's not a faithful rendering of the late 18th century, then the modern Venetians don't understand it. They'd ask us our plans, and when we explained our ideas, they would invariably say, 'But that's not Venetian!'"

"There were people," Dodie adds discreetly, "who said it wouldn't work, which was rather frightening in a way. And yet I had so much confidence in Tony and Hutton and even, I suppose, in myself that we were able to put aside those admonitions. And the very people who were telling us it wouldn't work have ended up liking it."

With the assistance of Venetian architect Franco Rosatto, the Duquette-Wilkinson makeover was accomplished in a miraculous (for Venice) eight months. Structural changes were few, and because walls for the most part couldn't be touched, much of the work to be done was purely decorative. The main salon retains its original wheat-colored linen, now slightly stained, and the walls of the grand ballroom have been embellished but not altered. The most dramatic change occurred in the master bedroom, which the designers lined with antique Chinese wallpaper. The hand-painted paper was from Pickfair, the famous Hollywood estate Duquette decorated in the 1940s for Mary Pickford. He had it flown in from L.A. and carefully mounted on panels that encircled

The elaborate stuccowork in the ballroom was done in the 19th century, while the raffia "branches" resembling coral are the work of Wilkinson and Duquette.

the room "like a giant Coromandel screen," Wilkinson notes.

Christmas 1998 was chosen as the target date for the Rosekrans family to celebrate their new life in Venice. And in mid-December, barges groaning under the weight of furniture both purchased from Venetian dealers and flown in from warehouses in San Francisco (Rosekrans) and Los Angeles (Duquette) progressed down the Grand Canal. The move took place as scheduled, though the public inauguration of the apartment wasn't until the following June, when the Rosekranses and the Brandolinis opened the palazzo for a grand ball to benefit the Venetian Heritage preservation association.

The startling result is pure theater. The historic grand ballroom has now become the Coral Ballroom, with thousands of raffia "coral" branches tucked into crevices in the intricate Rococo plasterwork and the Murano glass chandeliers and around the massive mirrors, paintings and putti adorning the doorways. The ballroom's banquettes have been reupholstered with silk brocade and trimmed with tiny coral "branches," each one made up of hundreds of orange beads handsewn by skilled Venetian fingers. Wilkinson commissioned three rust-and-gold-colored Venetian flags to fly off the balcony outside the ballroom, "because they add drama and movement," he says, to the already spectacular view.

The main salon, with its linen walls and four paintings in the style of Tiepolo that depict scenes from the lives of Antony and Cleopatra, has been lavished with tiger- and leopard-print silk velvets. Woven on 18th-century looms by the Venetian firm Bevilacqua, the fabrics cover chairs and pillows, hang at French doors and windows and even border the gold-framed canvases. The dining room, on the other hand, located just off the terrace, seems unearthed from Neptune's palace. The designers encrusted three Napoleon III mirrors with abalone shells and stag antlers, mounting them above antler-base consoles; San Francisco designer Andrew Fisher carried out much of the *coquillage* installation on site.

But the real achievement in the newest Rosekrans kingdom is that Duquette and Wilkinson created a setting of pure enchantment, in which the couple can do exactly what they love the most—entertain, in rooms that are as comfortable as they are inspired. To Dodie, the designers were not simply her creative team but keys to opening the doors of her life abroad. "They were able to create a world for me in which I flourish," she explains. "They understood the kind of life I enjoy living.

"Over all the years, John and I were making friends in different cities," she continues. "And that, to me, is very important, because a city, really any place in the world, would be a lonely place without friends."

VILLA WITH A VIEW

OVERLEAF: In Palm Beach, The Mezzacappas' Villa Venezia almost meets the Lake Worth sea wall in homage to the city of canals. "I am particularly fond of the way the house addresses the waterfront," says its architect, Jeffery Smith.

RIGHT: An arched colonnade gives way to the expansive living room. The walls are waxed Venetian plaster; the floor is cool terrazzo.

I

N JANUARY 2000, SHORTLY AFTER NEW YORKers Liz and Damon Mezzacappa had moved for the season into their striking new Venetian-style vacation house in Palm Beach, Florida, they gave a small dinner party. The doors of Villa Venezia's turquoise-walled dining room were open to the lantern-lit garden, with its whispering palms and the dark waters of Lake Worth beyond. Over the Italian walnut table, an extravagantly beaded Tuscan chandelier cast a soft light on the faces of the evening's dozen guests—key members of the local construction team, among them architect Jeffery Smith, contractor Hugh Davis and their spouses. Before dessert was served, Damon Mezzacappa toasted the assembled crowd by reading a poem he'd composed for the occasion. The unfolding rhymes captured with great comic flair every twist and turn of the long, exacting project—a five-year odyssey from the initial hunt for a suitable piece of land to the arrival of the last crates of hand-painted garden-bench tiles. Then he turned to his wife with a smile and concluded: "And Liz, thank you, too. After all, dear, you're one of the crew."

It was then that the room erupted in laughter. As is usually the case with the best jokes, Damon's kicker worked because it was grounded in truth: Liz had been a tireless toiler in pursuit of

perfection. Decorators and architects are often loath to share the credit. But in the case of Villa Venezia, every member of Liz's A-list creative team—which also included decorator Bunny Williams and landscape designer Deborah Nevins, both of New York—enthusiastically volunteered that she played an integral part in the design process. "Liz really worked hard," says Smith. "She came down here every two weeks during the two years of construction and sat through meetings upon meetings upon meetings." Adds Williams, who went on European buying trips with Liz and spent hours at her side hunting through antiques stores and thick auction catalogues for the perfect mix of Italian and Continental furnishings: "What's so great about Liz is that she's opinionated and has a completely clear vision. Plus, she really knows how to live in a house—she fills it up with interesting plates and napkins and flowers and, of course, people."

"Interesting" is the operative word when talking about Villa Venezia—named not just for its distinctive Italian style but in honor of Damon's late mother, Venezia Mezzacappa. When Palm Beach was first developed in the 1920s and '30s as a winter retreat for America's wealthiest families, the island's reigning architects of the day, Addison Mizner, Maurice Fatio and Marion Sims Wyeth, looked to the Mediterranean—primarily to Spain and Italy, with their comparable climates and wonderful light—for aesthetic inspiration. But they seldom employed the dramatic trefoil arches, delicate decorative stonework and truly audacious colors that are endemic to Venice.

"You've got to be careful with Venetian," admits Smith, the most adept young historicist working in Palm Beach today. (He's built Romanesque palazzi, Palladian villas, even a Shingle-style pile—but nothing before in the Venetian vernacular.) "Too much exuberance and the house starts to look like a wedding cake; too much restraint and the result is wishy-washy. But to her credit, Liz risked trying something different and ran with it." (She was so taken with the Venetian theme that she even named her wire-haired dachshund puppies Marco and Polo.)

The favorite architect of local homeowners Terry Allen Kramer, David and Julia Koch, Kathleen Ford and various members of the Lauder clan, Smith specializes in large houses that aren't victims of their own grandeur: unwieldy to live in, unpleasant to look at. For the Mezzacappas, he designed a house that is primarily composed of a two-story, H-shaped main block capped by a barreled, red-clay-tile roof. Upstairs, there are a pair of bedroom suites that are reached by a soaring stairwell; on the ground floor, a series of public rooms flow from a colonnaded central hallway. One end of the hallway opens onto a light-filled

garden room that in turn leads to a separate garage and guest wing. (And in a nod to the city of canals, the whole ensemble is pushed as close to the water's edge as local zoning would allow.)

Having already overseen the renovation of a Fifth Avenue apartment and the construction of a Southampton house, both relatively traditional in scope, Liz says she wanted to create a totally "magical and unique" retreat for the few months she'd be spending in Palm Beach every winter. (Damon, a financier, comes down for weekends and for longer stretches when his schedule permits.) "Because we live a somewhat formal life in New York," she explains, "we wanted a place that was relaxed, with doors always open to the wonderful smells of the garden."

If the house was conceived as an antidote to the strictures of New York City living, then the two-acre-plus garden was an outgrowth of the pleasure Liz derives from her Southampton property. She enlisted Deborah Nevins, with whom she had worked on Long Island, to create

house, Liz commissioned Smith to design an all-purpose garden room for Villa Venezia. With a rattan sofa Liz found in Bali as its centerpiece, the room has two long walls of French doors and a beamed ceiling lined in Indonesian straw. It has quickly become a favorite spot for reading and relaxing, as well as the site of many meals. "We rarely eat out in restaurants down here," Liz says. "But we eat everywhere in the house."

In fact, the Mezzacappas are just as likely to be found taking their meals in the library, the living room, the guest wing's media room or outside on the well-shaded loggia as they are in the dining room (whose turquoise and red hues are so dramatically delicious one wonders whether Bunny Williams chose them specifically to lure her clients back into the room). "We don't like to be predictable," Liz explains. "And you always have to learn how to make a house work in a way that suits your needs."

That means turning what was planned as an upstairs closet into a small office for Liz and her computer, and transforming what was to be a potting shed at the back of the guest wing into a third bedroom to accommodate the growing number of visiting grandchildren. Palm Beach life for the Mezzacappas may revolve around swimming, playing golf and enjoying the island's newly youthful energy, but Liz says it especially centers on entertaining family and friends.

a lush, exotic garden, full of fragrant star jasmine, shell ginger, gardenias and frangipani. "Liz really pushes for detail—the tile edging around the pool, the color of the gravel for her driveway," Nevins recounts. "Plus, she's originally from Australia, so she really knows her tropicals." Nevins selected such color-drenched plants as heliconias, Seminole hibiscus and bougainvillea, as well as "a seldom-used pale yellow oleander that looks fantastic against the apricot-pink walls of the house." There are stonework fountains (including one specifically designed for Marco and Polo to drink from), and, planted against the lakefront facade, two full-grown banyan trees that were brought over from West Palm Beach by barge.

And since she says she "lives in" the glass conservatory attached to her Southampton

The guest wing is where Liz and Williams really let loose—expanding on the Venetian theme and introducing North African and Middle Eastern elements into the decor. "As an important center of trade, Venice certainly absorbed these worldly influences into its design sensibility," Williams explains, adding with a laugh, "I'd also just returned from a wonderful vacation in Morocco when we started thinking about this part of the house." So bathrooms now have tiled Moorish niches, while the media room's decadently deep banquette, styled with a typically Moroccan wooden fringe, sits beneath a coffered cypress ceiling painted in lively saffron, teal and tomato red. "I've worked on a few houses by Mizner and Wyeth—and they required a certain amount of rigor," Williams explains. "But once Liz and Jeff had settled on the Venetian theme, it really opened things up for fun and fantasy."

Case in point: the unusual (albeit vintage Venice) terrazzo floor of the twenty-five-by-forty-five-foot main living room. "Usually, you'd see a wood or tile floor in Palm Beach," says Williams. Throughout the house, there are playfully overscaled mirrors, ornate cabinets, from India and elsewhere, built in as bars, and statuesque stone fireplaces made in the south of France.

These flights of fancy work, Williams concedes, because they're contained within such a controlled architectural envelope. "Jeff has the vocabulary and really understands details—the scale and proportions are always just right." Smith is an avid student of classical architecture as well as of more recent local precedents. "I love Fatio's work, which was more organized than Mizner's," he explains. "Mizner wanted his homes to look as if they'd been added on to over the years. I want them to look old, but not haphazard."

Smith says he'd always wanted to work in the Venetian vernacular and was thrilled to have finally found a sympathetic client. Now he and Liz are just patiently waiting to convince local authorities to allow them to put Venetian-style barber poles in the water (to moor the gondola, perhaps?). In fact, waiting is something Liz has become particularly good at during Villa Venezia's long journey to completion. "She's always willing to sit tight for unusual objects at the right scale," Williams explains. "Liz never says, 'Where is it, where is it?'"

And where is Liz? With the work finally done, she's now comfortably ensconced in an armchair on Villa Venezia's loggia, a lemonade in hand, the afternoon sun casting shadows through delicate stone tracery onto the coral-stone floor. "At this point, my duties have been reduced to in-house Maintenance Department," she says with a laugh, feigning complete exhaustion and looking out onto the calm water. "But I hope to retire soon from that job, too."

TWO FOR
THE TROPICS

I THINK WE CAN SAY THAT WE HAD THE BABY, AND then we got married."

Bunny Williams is a nice girl from Charlottesville, Virginia, who grew up to become one of this country's most esteemed decorators, so it stands to reason that her out-of-wedlock adventure a few years ago produced not a child but a house. What's surprising is that the building process, which for most couples is fractious at best, would in her case lead to both a new sanctuary in the Caribbean and marriage to its codesigner.

"This was something John and I could do together," Bunny explains, referring to her husband since 2004, antiques dealer John Rosselli. The two have known each other since the 1970s, when Bunny was a young associate at Parish-Hadley, New York's tastemaking decorating firm, and would pick through the inventory of John's Second Avenue shop every few weeks. They've been a couple since 1992 and are business partners in Treillage, a Manhattan garden store, as well. It's likely the shared parenting of that now-teenaged retail venture had almost as much to do with their marriage as dreaming up a new house did.

Whatever brought them together, the result is paradise as far as their friends are concerned, because Bunny and John share unimpeachable taste and the kind of generosity that turns

OVERLEAF: Luminous in the early-morning sunlight, the oceanfront porch off the great room holds chaise lounges designed by Oscar de la Renta.

LEFT: The house, designed by Ernesto Buch.

RIGHT: John often watches movies in the library, where antiques and objects from the natural world mix.

everyone around them into cherished companions. But more on that later.

Appropriately, their offspring is in paradise, or at least in one of the world's current versions of it: Punta Cana, a resort community on the southeastern tip of the Dominican Republic. Annual winter stays there with their good friends Annette and Oscar de la Renta had shown Bunny and John the sunny character of the place; the Dominican-born fashion designer is a partner in the oceanfront development. The enclave where the de la Rentas built their house in 1997 has mature palms, sea grapes, wild ginger and jacaranda all jostling to camouflage the well-endowed houses from view. You wouldn't guess that Oscar's friends Julio Iglesias and Mikhail Baryshnikov are just down the beach.

In 2003, the couple fell for three and a half acres just down the road, on a rise a short distance from the ocean. But before committing, Bunny and John came to terms with the fact that if they really wanted to spend a significant amount of time in Punta Cana, they would have to give up at least one of the other dwellings they'd managed to acquire, separately or together, over the years. Ultimately they decided to part with John's New Jersey farm and his town house in Savannah; they would keep Bunny's Colonial-era weekend retreat in Connecticut and their New York City apartment. They were confident that the friends and relations scat-

tered between New York and California would come to visit them in Punta Cana if invitations were extended. ("They really built the house to give themselves a new place to take their family and friends," explains Jonathan Gargiulo, John's nephew and alter ego in his antiques business.)

Flash forward two years. Bunny and John are sitting with a few of those friends on the terrace of La Colina ("the hill") after a late lunch, reliving some of the highlights of its short life. Their three dogs, all local adoptees, circle the table in hopes of a handout.

"Our first idea for the house was to build a Southern-style raised cottage," John says, bribing the dogs with butter cookies to stay on the porch as a hen and four chicks march across the front lawn. "Something you might see in Mississippi

355

or Georgia. We both respond to that style." (Mission accomplished—the flock crosses and scoots under a bayberry bush.)

"Then we got mixed up with Palladio—of course, John loves Palladio; they're both Italian—and we ended up combining the two," Bunny says. "We shared a philosophy of what we wanted: a house for entertaining, with great light, high ceilings and porches. It's never cold enough that you don't want to be outside."

"The property called for a large house," John interjects. "I don't know what he's saying—we had to build a large house to hold all of John's furniture from the other two places. John loves big furniture." Pause. "Of course, I do, too." Neither of them mentions that only a big house would do for all the near and dear arrayed across the country, waiting for their rooms to open up.

The couple worked on a plan with Ernesto Buch, a Cuban-American architect they'd known for some time, whose fluency in classical building styles they admired. Having designed the de la Rentas' house in Punta Cana, Ernesto knew the local contractors, and his New Haven office wasn't too far from Bunny's weekend place.

They quickly settled on a two-story, four-bedroom cottage of coquina, or coral stone, and hand-troweled stucco. It would have a single high-ceilinged great room on the second floor, with deep porches on either side that would face the ocean to the east and the less windy interior of the island to the west. In a nod to Thomas Jefferson she'd been wanting to make for decades, Bunny requested Monticello-style triple-hung windows that could double as doorways between the great room and its porches. Opening to a height of eight feet, these have proved to be so much fun to walk through that no one actually uses the French doors Ernesto included as an alternative. Just to the north of the main house, the architect designed a pool and a two-bedroom guesthouse that might just pass for a villa in the Veneto.

La Colina took nine months to plan and another eighteen to build. Starting in the spring of 2004, when ground was broken, Bunny came down about once a month. John often stayed in New York, but his absence didn't shield him from the wallet-emptying realities of construction.

First the couple discovered that the egregiously expensive copper gutters they needed hadn't been factored into the estimate. "They aren't used to working for people with budgets down here," John observes with deadpan accuracy. Next, they were told that they required two full feet of topsoil over the entire stony acreage if they wanted a garden. What would Bunny and John, not to mention the chickens, do without a garden? Then there was the roof. On one of her trips, Bunny saw the half-framed house peering down at her from its hillock and decided the

LEFT: "I don't really like looking at a pool from the main house—I'd rather have it be a separate destination," says Bunny. The cloistered swimming area includes a Palladian-style guesthouse with two bedrooms.

RIGHT: A family photo with Bubby, one of the couple's Dominican-born dogs.

peaked roof they'd planned would make the whole building too prominent—distinctly not what she'd had in mind. "So I borrowed the hipped roof from Drayton Hall, in Charleston."

The freewheeling nature of the Dominican building process was a novelty for Bunny, who found Ernesto's beautifully detailed plans filed in garbage bags during a particularly galling visit. "But once you have the baby, you forget the pain of childbirth," she says, in hibiscus-colored hindsight. "There isn't a day I don't walk around and feel in awe of the craftsmanship—and I love knowing it's handmade. Sometimes I think we have too much perfectionism in the States. Here there were very few tools involved."

Furnishing the new house was equally improvisational. John crated up his furniture from New Jersey and Savannah and shipped it to the nearest Dominican port. Bunny found places for everything. "I would have felt very disconnected had I not done that," John admits. "Your home has to represent who you are. Otherwise, it's ersatz and superficial."

Bunny enjoyed the freedom to compose rooms instinctually, without needing to sell a client on some of the more arcane relationships she created: a hulking hand-painted Sienese chest, for instance, beside a tufted armchair wearing a floral-printed linen. "This place was really about antidecorating," she says matter-of-factly.

Maybe so, but it lacks none of the qualities that make a house in the tropics delicious. "It's just Bunny and John, that house," says novelist Jane Stanton Hitchcock, a recent guest. "We'd go out during the day and then just long to get back to the house on the hill. It's that cozy comfort they do so well. Dogs, food and children are always part of the landscape."

The house came together as beautifully as Bunny and John did to the point that it should be no surprise that they married before the project was completed. They knew how it would turn out. And so, it seems, did their many friends and relations, who are no longer scattered between New York and California. They're all on their way to Punta Cana—or at least it seems that way to Bunny and John, who couldn't be happier.

359

HIDDEN HACIENDA

I N SEPTEMBER 2002 A HURRICANE PASSED THROUGH Mérida, the capital of Mexico's Yucatán state, downing power lines and causing flooding in a city much more accustomed to watching its eastern neighbors, Cancún and Cozumel, feel the effects of tropical storms. But hurricane Isidore was an exception. The Yucatán peninsula and parts of Mérida, including the office of governor Patricio Patron, were dark for days.

At a sprawling hacienda in the countryside, however, the reception rooms glowed like a length of amber beads. Dinner preparations carried on as usual, and even the underwater lights in the pool glimmered as high winds combed the acacia trees. The storm's only victims were some newly transplanted coconut palms behind the house, a former sisal plantation built in the 1860s.

Paula Cussi Azcárraga remembers the governor's calling to ask how she'd done it. "I told him I'd taken a lesson from my late husband," she says, sitting at an outdoor table set with after-dinner coffee and coconut cake sauced with rumpope, an eggnog-like liqueur made by local nuns. "Every time we bought a new house, he would put in his own generator. I just followed his advice."

At the time of his death, in 1997, Cussi's husband, Emilio Azcárraga, ran the Latin American television giant Grupo Televisa as well as a consortium of communications companies based in

In the dining room, Cussi has hung Anselm Keifer's painting *Sunflowers*, which towers over an 18th-century English mahogany table and chairs and an Indian cotton dhurrie. Three treasures populate the side table: a Trapani coral beaded cloth, a Mexican silver altarpiece and a painting by Giovanni del Biondo.

Mexico City and Los Angeles that had made him one of the wealthiest men on the continent. He and his wife kept houses in several countries and were among Mexico's first public patrons of contemporary art, with a museum that introduced the work of Roy Lichtenstein, Lucian Freud and Anselm Kiefer, among others, to Mexico City. When Azcárraga died, Cussi carried on doing all the things she enjoyed: exploring remote parts of the world with friends, collecting new artists and playing an active role on the boards of several museums, including the Metropolitan Museum and the Pompidou Center. As formidable as her husband was known to have been (his nickname was the Tiger), the vivacious blonde Cussi was clearly his match: the generator idea was as likely to have been hers from the start.

Since 2001, Cussi has found a new magnet for her energies in the Yucatán, a region better known for its hospitality to wild parakeets, spiny-tailed iguanas and tourists in Birkenstocks than a globe-trotting crowd of A-listers. With Cussi in residence, however, all that may change.

It was an invitation from a friend, the banker Roberto Hernandez, which first brought Cussi to the Yucatán in the late 1990s. Hernandez had bought several run-down haciendas near Mérida and restored them; Cussi was taken with the area's culture, its untouched forests and worn limestone hills. Before long she was in the real-estate market herself. The overwhelming majority of the haciendas she saw were built in the European styles favored by their owners, who had expatriated in the 19th century to participate in the booming sisal industry.

"The *hacendados* were so rich that they could afford to bring over architects and craftsmen from France and Italy," says Cussi, who met descendants of the colonial Péon clan during her search. The Péon relatives still owned two houses in Mérida—"bijoux French châteaus," Cussi calls them—and several haciendas; they were willing to part with the Italianate San Bernardo de Péon. (It is now San Bernardo de Cussi, in the local tradition.)

Cussi took one look at San Bernardo's great house, a single-story building with twenty-four-foot ceilings and verandas on three sides, and she envisioned a private art gallery. She called on a longtime collaborator, Guadalajara architect Marco Aldaco, to guide her. Aldaco made his name in the 1960s working for Noel and Gloria Guinness and later helped Gian Franco Brignone establish the resort of Careyes, whose architecture has been profoundly influential.

Here, Aldaco agreed with his patron that San Bernardo's warren of interior spaces could be opened up. He made the new center of the house a rectangular living room that spans its sixty-foot width; off one end is the library, and off the other are the dining room, kitchen and several reception

areas. A soaring interior gallery leads to a newly built bedroom suite and a private veranda for Cussi. Altogether, the residence amounts to fewer than ten centrally air-conditioned rooms. To make space for her guests—Cussi planned on changing a few minds about the Yucatán—Aldaco cleverly annexed the sisal factory, perpendicular to the main house, and laid out five guest suites opening onto an arcade. The factory's smokestack still juts into the sky—the only vertical gesture in a composition that mimics the relentless horizontality of the surrounding landscape.

Aldaco brought to the project a keen appreciation for Mayan craft traditions. He handpainted tiles for the bathrooms, cast small sculpted animals in gold for tabletop decorations and sketched a phantasmagoric mural that spans all three walls of Cussi's outdoor dining area. The idea for the mural originated with Susan Gutfreund, a New York decorator and a frequent partner on Cussi's global voyages. Gutfreund, who worked on the new interiors of San Bernardo

OVERLEAF: "I adore celadon," says Cussi, whose bedroom suite (both pages) revolves around the color and paintings by Lee Krasner (left) and Lucian Freud (right).

LEFT: A pool and dining terrace adjoin the guest wing, whose smokestack recalls its industrial past.

RIGHT: Cussi by the pool with her dog Shatoosh.

from their inception, recalls visiting the hacienda while it was still under renovation.

"Paula and I were having dinner out on the veranda one night, and I felt the walls needed something. I thought a tapestry would be wonderful. Paula said, 'Susan, you're nuts! It would take twenty years to weave!' So Marco offered to draw us a mural."

Gutfreund had other good ideas. After spotting locally woven hammocks at a gift shop in Uxmal, she marched back to the hacienda with a plan: she would use the woven twine to make curtains, effecting couture macramé.

"But first she had to find the weavers," Cussi recalls. "Susan never faltered—she headed right into the little Indian village here and found the women to do the job. It may have taken three tries, but the curtains are divine." Other elements Gutfreund commissioned were a little longer in transit, including a custom-woven Indian dhurrie for the dining room, furniture from Morocco for the verandas and rush matting for the living room, plaited in Scotland. But when all the ingredients finally coalesced, the results were exactly what the 21st-century *hacendada* had in mind: a new concept for a Yucatán domestic tradition.

Cussi bought little for San Bernardo beyond Gutfreund's selections. She curated her possessions to suit the new setting. In addition to an important collection of paintings, she

has one of the country's top holdings of early Mexican furniture, as well as Latin American religious art and treasures from a lifetime of trolling antiques fairs. Though populating the hacienda with these things wasn't a straightforward process, it was a gratifying one that resulted in some highly charged combinations.

Cussi now spends about eight months out of twelve in the Yucatán and her friends are beginning to visit. "People always ask whether they can bring me something when they come," she says, her eyebrows shooting up in disbelief. For goodness' sake, we have Costco, Home Depot and Sky TV. You can watch Sky TV in the Mayan forest!"

"The beauty of the Yucatán is that you are isolated, but you are not isolated," she continues, falling headlong back into her new favorite subject.

369

DESIGN FORUM
BUILDING A HOUSE FROM AFAR

Architect Donald Rattner and interior designer Victoria Hagan collaborated on a new house at the Greenbrier resort, in the West Virginia hills.

The dream of building your own house in the next great place—whether it be the islands, the mountains, the woodlands or out West—is a shared one among *Town & Country* readers, and one many of them have fulfilled. It's never easy. Patience and focus are essential when you're supervising the design, construction and decoration of a house long-distance; the same is true when you're simply overhauling an existing home to suit your own tastes or customizing a house within a planned resort development.

DUE DILIGENCE
Before you close on a new piece of land far from home, there are two kinds of questions you should be asking.

■ Question your broker or a local real-estate attorney on the governing rules concerning new-house size, height and neighborhood density, and about any relevant zoning issues. Though you may chafe against rules that are intended to minimize visual conflict, they do tend to maximize property values and liquidity, two selling points for vacation homes in the first place.

■ Ask current homeowners how strict the regulatory climate can be. Is there an architectural review board to be aware of? An environmental review board? While these organizations can feel restrictive in some situations, when it comes to a second home, context and the relationship between the built environment and the natural world are enormously important issues.

CASE STUDY: CUSTOMIZING A NEW HOUSE
When Solé and Nick Riley bought a house in a new development underway in the Hamptons, the design of the simple contemporary house of 4,500 square feet was almost complete. The architect was New York–based Annabelle Selldorf. Still, the couple wanted to put their own stamp on their second home. Working with Selldorf and the builder for the development, they were able to customize

The 4,500-square-foot Greenbrier
house took twelve months to build.
It was partly inspired by Adirondack-
style architecture.

ABOVE: *The warm palette of the Greenbrier living room reveals the care Victoria Hagan put into linking the decor with its wooded surroundings.*

RIGHT: *When she designed this master bedroom, Hagan could only imagine what the view would be: she imagined treetops and sky.*

the interior in minor but satisfying ways. They chose special glass tile for the bathrooms, selected kitchen appliances and finishes and had their say on flooring—stone on the first floor, wood on the second. Such changes are usually well within the realm of possibility—you only have to ask, and be ready to say which customizations on your list are the most important to you.

YOUR TEAM

Keep in mind that the success or failure of your project will be in the hands of the team you assemble to help you. Any long-distance building project demands unbroken communication for months and often years, and participants need to think of themselves as collaborators. Architect, designer and contractor must be able to work together without resorting to infighting or political maneuvering.

THE ARCHITECT

When hiring an architect, going local isn't important—talent and professionalism are. A small percentage of the design work will be done on site, and as long as the architect understands local conditions and is familiar with the chosen materials, you're set. Certain parts of the country require that a state-certified architect sign off on residential plans, and if so, your architect can arrange to have that done.

THE INTERIOR DESIGNER

Consider hiring an interior designer as a member of your project team if you're building from scratch, even if the house will just be a part-time getaway. When you're building at some distance, the house is basically an abstraction to you until the day you move in. Good designers are attuned to countless details you wouldn't necessarily think about, much less articulate to an architect in the planning stages. And even the most conscientious architect can benefit from a designer's insights on matters like efficient pantry layout, tub and window placement in a bathroom and smart deployment of electrical outlets in a child's room. As with

Morocco has age-old methods of wall
decoration, which Kenyon Kramer
and Jean-Louis Raynaud utilized when
restoring this Marrakech house.

architects, a designer's talent is more important than his or her location. If anything, designer and architect should be in proximity to each other and to you, since you'll collaborate with them in the design phase.

THE CONTRACTOR

When hiring the contractor, going local is best. The firm will understand local codes—and often the people behind the codes—building conditions and the best sources for materials in the area. If your site or your design is challenging, then it's helpful to wait until you have architectural plans in hand to retain the contractor. That way the specific challenges of your project can be taken into account when hiring. Refinements to the plan can be made after the builder is on board.

A CONSTRUCTION ADMINISTRATOR
AND/OR OWNER'S REPRESENTATIVE

The final roles you may want to cast are that of personal watchdogs to oversee your project. A residence of significant size (say 8,000-plus square feet) should have a construction administrator to ensure that the architect's plans are adhered to on site. This is a role established architects provide (usually for an added five percent fee) along with their design services; it involves regular site visits by a project architect. If your house is on a major scale or very remote, you might also consider hiring an owner's representative who will act in your best interests as a facilitator and a mediator between team members if necessary, cutting down on the time you spend managing— and traveling back and forth to the distant job site.

CASE STUDY:
A HOUSE AT THE GREENBRIER RESORT

Interior designer Victoria Hagan worked with architect Donald Rattner on a woodland home at the Greenbrier resort in West Virginia a few years ago, and they both benefited from the partnership. Hagan explains why such a

A lakeside house in Guatamala designed by John Herrera of New York City features a playful modernist staircase of wood and stone.

The traditional brickwork used in this vaulted ceiling in Marrakech became the focus of the outdoor living area. Metal lanterns draw the eye upward.

collaboration is useful. "In the design phase," she says, "we can discuss the relationship of spaces, the quality of light we're each envisioning. We can have a dialogue about the size of the windows. 'What about adding one here?' I can ask. 'Can we have a transom window there? What will that do to the facade?' We can consider the progression of rooms, what it will be like to travel through the spaces, and we can modulate them. Donald sees that progression architecturally, and I see it in a more tangible way—how color, textures and materials can enhance the mood and the architecture." "The decorating only comes through in the last six months," Victoria Hagan says. "The real point I'm making is this: I'm a good fixer, but why pay a designer to craft Band-Aids when you can have a healthy house right from the beginning?"

GETTING THE HOUSE YOU WANT

The journey will never be as straight as you want it to be when designing and building a home from afar, but taking these five steps into account before you begin will help you end up in a good place.

■ In your initial meetings, brief your architect and your designer about how you plan to live in the new setting. Will someone in the family be taking up a new hobby that requires its own space (painting, fly tying, orchid growing)? Will you be entertaining more, or less? Will weekend guests be a given? Will your kids soon be teenagers and want to have their own floor?

■ Once your team is in place and the job gets underway, regular communication among you and all the team members will help things stay on track. Scheduled conference calls can keep even the most far-flung project moving. Calls might be weekly during the design phase, and weekly or even daily during parts of the construction phase. Participants should include the chief contractor, the architect, the designer, any consultants whose work is underway (engineering, lighting, media, landscape), and the owner or owner's rep.

■ Don't forget to make the computer a part of your team. Together, digital photography and e-mail have revolutionized long-distance building. The owner can have an accurate sense of just how far along the project is without hopping on a plane.

■ That said, site visits are essential. Plan to make several: when the foundation is staked but not yet dug, to confirm your siting choice; once the framing is done, to check on views from various windows, room dimensions and the like; and before the walls are closed up, your last opportunity to make inexpensive changes to the plumbing and electrical plans. Only site visits will suffice.

■ Whether you're working on a grand scale or not, a final piece of advice is this: make sure you allow enough time for the professionals you've chosen to do their jobs. A house any bigger than a beach shack should be given at least eighteen months to build and furnish. Delays due to weather conditions and late delivery of materials are inevitable—accept that from the beginning, and you won't lose (as much) sleep.

CASE STUDY: A HOUSE IN THE TROPICS

When New York City decorator Bunny Williams was building a getaway for herself and her husband, John Rosselli, from scratch in the Dominican Republic, she drew on the knowledge she'd picked up on previous visits to stay with friends. Her understanding of the island's vernacular building styles helped immensely when it came time for her to choose materials; she went with stucco for the facade and interior walls, knowing that the local craftsmen could apply it by hand with expert skill (the same can no longer be said in the United States). She knew of a factory on the island still making cement tile in vintage patterns she loved; Williams was able to work with the factory to custom-color a number of batches for her personal use. These details make the house inimitably suit—and reflect—its surroundings, a noble and attainable goal for any residence.

The hand-stuccoed walls of Bunny Williams's ground-floor porch are crisply detailed, thanks to fine Dominican craftsmanship.

PHOTO CREDITS

Page 2 Oberto Gili; *The Sheaf, 1953*: © 2010 Succession H.
   Matisse / Artists Rights Society (ARS), New York
Page 4 Oberto Gili
Page 8 Fernando Bengoechea/Beateworks/Corbis
Page 10 Fernando Bengoechea
Pages 14–33 Oberto Gili
Pages 34–42 William Abranowicz/Art + Commerce
Pages 44–57 Dean Kaufman
Pages 58–61 Fernando Bengoechea/Beateworks/Corbis
Pages 62–64 Fernando Bengoechea
Pages 66–67 Fernando Bengoechea/Beateworks/Corbis
Pages 68–69 Fernando Bengoechea
Page 70 Fernando Bengoechea/Beateworks/Corbis
Pages 72–80 William Abranowicz/Art + Commerce
Pages 82–89 Matthew Hranek/Art + Commerce
Pages 90–96 Oberto Gili
Pages 98–104 James Merrell
Pages 106–112 Jim Wright/Icon International
Page 115 Fernando Bengoechea
Page 116 Marianne Haas
Page 117 Oberto Gili
Page 118 Oberto Gili
Page 119 Fernando Bengoechea
Page 120 Maura McEvoy
Page 121 Michael Mundy
Page 122 Fernando Bengoechea
Pages 124–125 Fernando Bengoechea/Beateworks/Corbis
Pages 127–131 Fernando Bengoechea
Pages 132–133 Fernando Bengoechea/
   Beateworks/Corbis
Page 134 Fernando Bengoechea
Pages 136–149 Christopher Simon Sykes
Pages 150–161 Maura McEvoy
Pages 162–166 ©SKREBNESKI
Pages 168–169 Gilles de Chabaneix
Page 170 Richard Bowditch
Pages 173 Gilles de Chabaneix
Pages 174–182 Dean Kaufman
Pages 184–195 Laura Resen
Pages 196–204 Anita Calero
Pages 206–212 Ngoc Minh Ngo
Page 214 Maura McEvoy

Page 215 Maura McEvoy
Page 216 Don Freeman
Page 217 Oberto Gili
Page 218 Marc Royce
Page 219 Marc Royce
Page 220 Art Streiber/August
Page 221 Maura McEvoy
Pages 222–233 Oberto Gili; *Sigmund Freud & Franz Kafka*
   on page 222: © 2010 The Andy Warhol Foundation for
   the Visual Arts, Inc./Artists Rights Society (ARS), New
   York and Courtesy Ronald Feldman Fine Arts, New
   York/www.feldmangallery.com; *Abstract Composition
   of a Young Girl* on page 231: © 2010 Donald Baechler/
   Artists Rights Society (ARS), New York
Pages 234–235 Fernando Bengoechea/Beateworks/Corbis
Pages 237–243 Fernando Bengoechea
Pages 244–253 Oberto Gili
Pages 254–265 Oberto Gili
Pages 266–274 Oberto Gili
Pages 276–279 Matthew Hranek
Pages 280–281 Matthew Hranek/Art + Commerce
Pages 282–285 Matthew Hranek
Pages 286–290 Michael Mundy
Pages 292–301 Oberto Gili
Page 303 Fernando Bengoechea
Page 304 Francesco Lagnese
Page 305 Brian Doben
Page 306 Brian Doben
Page 307 Matthew Hranek
Page 308 Oberto Gili
Page 309 Thomas Loof
Pages 310–323 Paul Costello
Pages 324–327 Fernando Bengoechea/Beateworks/Corbis
Page 328 Fernando Bengoechea
Pages 329–335 Fernando Bengoechea/Beateworks/Corbis
Pages 336–346 Matthew Hranek/Art + Commerce
Pages 348–358 Fritz von der Schulenberg
Page 359 Brian Doben
Pages 360–369 Maura McEvoy
Pages 370–373 Maura McEvoy
Page 374 Oberto Gili
Page 375 Fernando Bengoechea
Page 376 Paul Costello
Page 377 Fritz von der Schulenberg

INDEX

HEARST BOOKS
New York

An Imprint of Sterling Publishing
387 Park Avenue South
New York, NY 10016

This book was previously published as a hardcover.

Library of Congress Cataloging-in-Publication Data
At home with Town & country / from the editors of Town & country
magazine.
    p. cm.
 Includes index.
1. Architecture, Domestic. 2. Interior decoration. 3. Lifestyles. I. Town &
country (New York, N.Y.) II. Title: At home with Town and country.
 NA7120.A75 2008
 747—dc22
                     2007047739

10 9 8 7 6 5 4 3 2 1

Town & Country is a registered trademark of Hearst Communications, Inc.

www.townandcountrymag.com

For information about custom editions, special sales, premium and
corporate purchases, please contact Sterling Special Sales Department at
800-805-5489 or specialsales@sterlingpublishing.com.

Distributed in Canada by Sterling Publishing
c/o Canadian Manda Group, 165 Dufferin Street
Toronto, Ontario, Canada M6K 3H6

Distributed in Australia by Capricorn Link (Australia) Pty. Ltd.
P.O. Box 704, Windsor, NSW 2756 Australia

Manufactured in China

Sterling ISBN 978-1-58816-988-4

DESIGNED BY MARY SHANAHAN AND EFFIE TSU

Front Cover credits:

All images on front cover by Oberto Gili except:

Far left, top: Fernando Bengoechea

Top, center column: Dean Kaufman

Far right, top: Dean Kaufman

Far right, middle: Thomas Loof

Far right, bottom: Fernando Bengoechea

Front Inside Flap credits:

Top: Oberto Gili

Bottom: Thomas Loof

Back Cover credits:

All images on back cover by Oberto Gili except:

Far left, top: Maura McEvoy

Far right, top: Fernando Bengoechea

Far right, middle: Oberto Gili; *Sigmund Freud & Franz Kafka*:
    © 2010 The Andy Warhol Foundation for the Visual Arts, Inc./
    Artists Rights Society (ARS), New York and Courtesy Ronald
    Feldman Fine Arts, New York/www.feldmangallery.com

Far right, bottom: Christopher Simon Sykes

Far left, bottom: Fernando Bengoechea

Far left, middle: Christopher Simon Sykes

Back Inside Flap credits:

All images: Oberto Gili